DILY GUIDEPOSTS

·····················

25 DEVOTIONS FOR ADVENT

EDITORS OF GUIDEPOSTS

Guideposts

New York

■ **ZONDERVAN**®

ZONDERVAN

Daily Guideposts: 25 Devotions for Advent
Copyright © 2016 by Guideposts

Requests for information should be addressed to:
Zondervan, *3900 Sparks Dr. SE, Grand Rapids, Michigan 49546*

ISBN 978-0-310-34925-9 (softcover)

ISBN 978-0-310-34943-3 (ebook)

Bible translations quoted in this book are listed on page 57, which
hereby becomes a part of this copyright page.

Any Internet addresses (websites, blogs, etc.) and telephone numbers
in this book are offered as a resource. They are not intended in
any way to be or imply an endorsement by Zondervan, nor does
Zondervan vouch for the content of these sites and numbers for the
life of this book.

Cover design: Müllerhaus
Cover photo: Shutterstock°
Interior design: Kait Lamphere

First printing August 2016 / Printed in the United States of America

Season's greetings, friend!

When the nights start getting longer and the cold wind whips around our ankles, there are lots of things we start putting on: woolen socks and scarves, hats and gloves, sweaters and jackets. We head out to the stores and put shopping bags, filled with gifts for loved ones, on our arms. We throw a log on the fire and put up colorful strings of lights outside because they look lovely and hold back the night just a bit.

As Paul points out in Romans 13:14, all the things we put on this time of year can make it hard to clothe ourselves with Christ. Jesus, born into this world as light in the darkness, is the reason that love, forgiveness, redemption, and hope have the final say.

God desires to come to us in the midst of our lives. Mary was busy going about her daily work, when the angel Gabriel told her she would conceive and give birth to a son, whom she would name Jesus. Mary's response? "How will this be . . . since I am a virgin?" And then, "May your word to me be fulfilled" (Luke 1:26–38, NIV).

So for the next twenty-five days, join us as we put on the light, one candle at a time. We remind ourselves to take off those things that we do not need and wrap ourselves in what is coming: the Light of the World.

This is the season of Advent, a time of wonder and anticipation, a time to ponder the miracle and mystery of Christ's birth.

Blessings,
Editors of Guideposts

DECEMBER 1

THE CROSSLET

Out of Zion, the perfection of beauty,
God will shine forth. —Psalm 50:2 *(NKJV)*

In the early 1970s, Bea Alexander told our churchwomen's group about the most beautiful tree she'd ever seen—a "Chrismon tree." The pictures of exquisitely crafted white-and-gold ornaments on a stately balsam tree were breathtaking. Bea said that Frances Kipps Spencer of Danville, Virginia, had created the ornaments, which were all symbols of the Christian faith, to remind people of the true meaning of Christmas.

We voted unanimously to replicate the tree in our small church and immediately ordered the pattern book and kits. Despite the fact that I'm all thumbs, I agreed to make three ornaments. Reality hit two weeks later when I received a bag of wire, pearls, foam, and gold trim to make a "Latin crosslet," the symbol for perfection.

I tried, but my ornament bore only a vague resemblance to the picture. "What a joke!" I lamented to the pastor's wife. "My crosslet is about as far from perfect as possible."

She examined the crosslet, then said, "It's a bit lopsided, and the beads aren't spaced right. But that's beside the point. The Chrismon tree isn't about perfect craftsmanship. It's about Jesus."

My crosslet was among the ornaments on our tree the first Sunday of Advent, along with my two less-than-perfect stars placed on the back of the tree. The flaws would hardly be noticeable to the people sitting in the pews. In fact, they made the tree more special. Our congregation of imperfect people entered the season of preparation with an imperfect but beautiful tree inviting us to a deeper faith in our perfect Savior.

Beautiful Savior, may every symbol of Your birth draw us closer to You. —Penney Schwab

Digging Deeper: *Ecclesiastes 3:11; Philippians 3:12*

DECEMBER 2

MAKING CHRISTMAS

"A new spirit will I put within you."
—*Ezekiel 36:26 (KJV)*

Christmas was creeping up on me and I was so busy basking in the year's successes in my financial consulting business that I hadn't given the holiday much thought. I tallied up my clients' gains and muttered "well done" under my breath as I shut down my computer.

That night I had dinner with some associates. "This is what it's all about," I said as I made a toast to the group. Everyone nodded in agreement.

The next day, I headed to the mall. Carols were blaring through the speakers as people bustled about, but I felt empty.

The next morning I pulled up behind the line of cars parked on my parents' street. Every December my family hosts a Christmas brunch, mostly for people who have no family or no place to go. *Why can't it just be us?* I wished as I walked through the front door. I breathed in the smell of country ham and baking biscuits. Kate, who had never missed one of these gatherings, was leaning on her walker near the fireplace, watching my niece Abby playing with her new doll. In the kitchen my mother was laughing as she dished out the cheese grits.

I recognized it first on the faces of the people gathered around her. It spread through the house and finally it filled up my heart—the spirit of Christmas, the biggest dividend of all. And in that moment I understood that investing in people is a lot more important than investing for them.

Father, You invested everything in us when You sent us Your Son. Fill me with Your spirit as I invest myself in Your people. —Brock Kidd

Digging Deeper: *Matthew 25:35–40; James 1:27*

December 3

Turn Aside

Get the truth and never sell it;
also get wisdom, discipline, and
good judgment. —Proverbs 23:23 *(NLT)*

The commercial countdown began weeks ago, and today advertisements tell us how many shopping days until Christmas. In other words, spend! Buy! Get ready!

However, the coming weeks also provide precious opportunity to do some spiritual spending, and the Bible gives an interesting shopping list: truth, wisdom, discipline, and good judgment.

During this hectic season, what I need to seek as doggedly as I search the stores or the Internet for those "perfect gifts" of toys, books, and clothing is God's wisdom. It seems no coincidence that discipline is next on the list! Too often I've seen a connection between lack of discipline in my life and a shortage of understanding how to love God and the people around me. This Advent I want to establish a small discipline of taking a few quiet moments each day to think about Jesus, the Wisdom of God. Who is He? Who can He be for me?

Even in this busy time, God wants to come to me in the midst of my everyday life. Moses was busy going about his daily work, tending sheep on Mount Horeb, when he came upon an incredible sight: the Angel of the Lord appearing in a flame of fire from the midst of a bush. Moses's response? "I will now turn aside and see this great sight" (Exodus 3:3, NKJV).

God, a consuming fire, comes as an infant in a virgin's womb! The season of Advent isn't enough even to begin to ponder His appearance, but I want to try—to turn aside and gaze on Him a bit more each day.

Lord, help me to acquire Your wisdom and better understand who You are. —Mary Brown

Digging Deeper: *Psalm 46:10; Proverbs 4:7*

The Promise Fulfilled

"But you, Bethlehem Ephrathah, though you are little among the thousands of Judah, yet out of you shall come forth to Me the One to be Ruler in Israel, whose goings forth are from of old, from everlasting." —Micah 5:2 (NKJV)

"Let's try there," Margi said, "over that hill." My wife pointed up a steep incline. Three families trekked through knee-deep snow somewhere in the rugged woods of northern California. Armed with a permit, we searched for that most elusive quarry: the perfect Christmas tree. It had become our post-Thanksgiving family tradition.

Each year, hot chocolate and strong coffee fueled our two-hour drive into the snowcapped peaks of the national forests. The kids scrambled up the snowy hillside. The adults struggled along. Nobody complained. Tall pines frosted with snow, a cobalt sky, and rugged terrain made for a postcard vista. Add the laughter of children and a few snowball fights, and nothing could have been better.

"How about this one?" someone shouted.

"No, the back is bare."

"Or that one? Or the next one?"

My aching legs wanted us to settle for something scrawny, but I bit back my whining.

"I think the perfect tree is always going to be over the next hill," my daughter, Josie, said.

"Well, that's just where we'll have to go," Margi responded.

That's how hope is, I thought. It's a promise fulfilled over the next hill. Generations abided in Christ before Christ came. They pressed forward in hope, finding that confidence in future grace is never disappointed.

The next hill paid off. Our tree was perfect. Just like the Savior.

Lord, You promised a Savior and He came. As I trudge through life, may I rest my heart in future grace, perfectly fulfilled in Him. —Bill Giovannetti

Digging Deeper: *Luke 2:1–6*

DECEMBER 5

MAKING ROOM

"Then shall the virgin rejoice in the dance, both young men and old together: for I will turn their mourning into joy, and will comfort them, and make them rejoice from their sorrow." —Jeremiah 31:13 (KJV)

We live in the smallest house in the neighborhood. Actually, we may live in the smallest house in several neighborhoods. Sandee and I moved here BK (before kids) and referred to our tiny abode as "our starter home." That was twenty-five years and three kids ago. Whatever we were supposed to start is surely finished by now.

Five people in a small house is—well— intimate. I can honestly say that I learned more about my three daughters' daily habits than I wanted to, and I'm sure they'd say the same about me. I have seen my kids stand on the porch in a driving rainstorm, just to have some privacy on the phone. I gleefully volunteered for shopping duty—even the crowded grocery store had more room than my kitchen.

Now it's Christmastime and they're all home again, plus some out-of-town guests, so one or more kids will sleep on the floor or couch. You'd think this would lead to conflicts—in a house this small, we've had our share of those—but it's mostly (and surprisingly) peaceful. There is a lot of laughter, a lot of screaming (usually lyrics to the B-52s), a lot of what loosely would be labeled dancing.

And having survived on this small island for twenty-five years, isolated with four others in the primitive tribe, I happily join the natives in dance. Turns out, it doesn't require much space to make a family . . . couple walls, really, or maybe a barn if there's no other place. I'm sure someone will sleep on the floor if that's what it takes to make room this season.

Lord, sometimes my home is crowded and my heart is not open. Let me learn how to make more room in both.
—Mark Collins

Digging Deeper: *Romans 12:16–18*

December 6

The Bright Morning Star

And there were shepherds living out in the fields nearby, keeping watch over their flocks at night. —Luke 2:8 (NIV)

On the night Jesus was born, I can picture the shepherds watching their flocks with single-minded devotion. This was their most important job. Once night fell, perhaps it was their only job. The wise men watched the skies with the same intensity. Nothing was more important than determining the location of this new king's birth.

Watching the sheep, watching a star, watching and waiting with a singular focus. Quite different from life in the twenty-first century when I think of all I find myself watching in a typical Christmas season. I watch my husband Paul's men's choir concert and watch for sales on decorations and the gifts on my list. We watch our neighbor dance in the annual production of *The Nutcracker*, and watch our favorite TV specials like *A Charlie Brown Christmas*. Then there's the church concert and a movie or two—after all, would it be Christmas without *Miracle on 34th Street*?

Watching all this makes for a busy season but doesn't necessarily keep my focus on Jesus. Even church concerts and Christmas shows, while carrying the message of Christ's birth, can distract me from focusing on Christ Himself. So I've begun a new habit this Advent. Each evening I walk out my back door and, taking a cue from the wise men, scan the December sky for the brightest object—Sirius, the Dog Star. I watch it for a few moments, and not only do I feel connected to that first Christmas, but it's time each night to focus my heart on the One at the center of it all.

Jesus, You are the bright morning star. Lead me to make You the center of every Christmas season.
—Gina Bridgeman

Digging Deeper: *Isaiah 9:2; Colossians 1:17*

DECEMBER 7

MAKING TIME

The voice of one crying in the wilderness,
Prepare ye the way of the Lord, make his
paths straight. —Matthew 3:3 (KJV)

Almost like clockwork, on the second Sunday of Advent I'd start making excuses about why I didn't have time to write letters or personal notes inside my Christmas cards. I know Advent is the time we reach out to all our loved ones, but by this time of year I'm often complaining that I don't even have time to buy, sign, seal, and send the cards themselves, never mind writing a personal note in each one.

Then a friend suggested, "Tell yourself that you only have to write three personal notes a day. Figure out how many loved ones you want to touch with a personal greeting and start writing the cards in September if you have to."

That year I wrote over three dozen letters.

I did it by finding lots of little twenty-minute chunks of time: waiting for the roast to finish cooking or the clothes to finish drying; sitting in the doctor's or dentist's office; during the commercials of my favorite TV show; while enjoying my morning cup of tea.

I used to look at that pile of Christmas cards and shudder. Now I divide the task into small, manageable bites of two or three letters a day. Before I know it, I'm heading to the post office, job completed.

This year I'm sending twenty-four Christmas letters to friends and family around the country. I'm writing three letters a day. In eight days I'll be finished. And this year my letters are going to include reasons the person I'm writing to is so special to me.

Isn't that what Advent is all about? Building up others so their hearts expand enough to also welcome the Christ Child into their lives on a daily, permanent basis?

Heavenly Father, as I write personal notes to my loved ones this Advent, help me to help them see how You are a very real presence in our lives. —Patricia Lorenz

Digging Deeper: *1 Thessalonians 5:11; Hebrews 10:24*

....

DECEMBER 8

READING THE WORD

"See, I am coming soon . . . I am the Alpha and the Omega, the first and the last, the beginning and the end." —Revelation 22:12–13 (NRSV)

"Daddy, let me find it." I handed my well-worn pocket version of the New Testament and Psalms to Timothy. His small fingers thumbed through the pages for a passage in Revelation he'd learned in Sunday school. "This!" he said triumphantly. Then he read in a firm, clear voice, "'I am the Alpha and the Omega, the first and the last, the beginning and the end.' That's my favorite verse."

"Why do you like it?" I asked. Was it because

it mirrored the challenge of remembering what letters went first in his spelling words, like the e or the i in receive or neighbor? Or maybe it was the dawning awareness of who was first and who was last in school tests and playground contests.

"It's just so big," he said. We got off the subway, and as we walked to his school I made a little speech about how Jesus had come and would come back and that we were in this period of both celebrating His coming and awaiting His return, that He was both in time and outside of time, a little like a sci-fi movie. "And we pray for His kingdom on earth to come as we prepare for Christmas."

Timothy walked in silence for a moment, then said, "But He's here now and He's everything. The Alpha, the Omega, the beginning, and the end."

"Yes," I said, "exactly."

"Bye, Daddy," he said, running to catch up with some friends. It made me think I would be running to catch up with him for the rest of his life.

Jesus is here now. Why didn't I put it that way? The beginning and end and everything in between.

Dear Lord, we await Your coming like we await the arrival of a best friend who is already here. —Rick Hamlin

Digging Deeper: *Psalm 118:22*

....

DECEMBER 9

LEARNING TO GIVE

> *He that hath mercy on the poor,*
> *happy is he.* —Proverbs 14:21 *(KJV)*

"Oh boy," I mumbled under my breath as my son, Harrison, and I walked into the mall. Maybe I was in over my head this time. In an effort to teach Harrison about the importance of giving, we had adopted a needy family for Christmas. The father was in prison and the mother was working three jobs, trying to make ends meet. Her son was Harrison's age and her daughter was a few years younger. The mother's earnings were meager, and there was little money for presents.

On the ride over, I had done the best I could to

explain things to Harrison. But walking into the store was like stepping into an instant replay of the commercials we had seen while watching Saturday morning cartoons. The shelves were groaning with things that seemed designed to fill the purest heart with greed. In an atmosphere like that, how could a seven-year-old grasp the concept of giving?

"Hey, Daddy," Harrison said gleefully, "that boy would love this game. It will make him so happy! And isn't the little sister Abby's age? [Abby was his cousin.] She'll love this doll and those books over there!"

I could feel my heart warming.

"What about the mom? I think she'd like some new clothes and maybe a purse." Before we knew it, our shopping cart was full.

But my best present ever was waiting in the checkout lane. Harrison insisted on unloading the cart himself. With a faraway look in his eyes, he picked up each item and placed it carefully on the counter. He lingered for a moment over the last item and then he turned to me and looked straight into my eyes. "Jesus is right, Daddy," he said. "It is better to give than to get."

Father, thanks for letting me glimpse Your Son's wisdom with my son's eyes. —Brock Kidd

Digging Deeper: *Acts 20:35; Luke 6:38*

....

DECEMBER 10

MERCIFUL LOVE

"To you is born this day in the city of David a Savior, who is the Messiah, the Lord." —Luke 2:11 (NRSV)

I was cleaning out drawers in advance of my daughter's Christmas fly-in from college and came across several homemade coupon books Lulu gave me when she was younger. Each set was handcrafted—one with shiny hearts, another speckled with stars—and her handwriting evolved with the years.

Initially, they were generous: helping me in the garden or setting the table twenty-five times, being nice fifteen times, leaving me alone twelve times. "This card is good for making me _____," one said. She promised love-feats beyond her talents even today, as a college student: cooking five dinners, for example.

Redeeming the coupons that first year proved burdensome, so the next year she promised less: letting me brush her hair two times, for example. Still, she worried I might overuse the coupons or use one after she'd forgotten her promises. So she set strict expiration dates and issued me a stamp and stamp pad for keeping track.

I never thought to use any except when she was mad and thus unlikely to make good on them. And really, all I've ever wanted from her is what God wants from us: love.

One coupon I especially cherish promises just that: "Good for being loved on. No limits! Never expires!"

That's God's Christmas coupon every year.

Father God, thank You for Your merciful love that ignores our faults and promises us delights beyond what we can imagine. —Patty Kirk

Digging Deeper: *Jeremiah 31:3; 1 John 4:10*

DECEMBER 11

KNOWING THE LIGHT

That was the true Light, which lighteth every man
that cometh into the world. —John 1:9 *(KJV)*

I'm an amateur mechanic. My automotive
repairs don't always conform to daylight hours,
so I have mastered the flashlight-in-the-mouth
look. Sometimes a trouble light just won't fit, so
I cram a small penlight between my teeth and
slide underneath the car.

Seems pretty primitive, right? Let me
tell you: In ancient times, a guy with a mini-
flashlight would be worshipped as a deity. All
they had in the darkness was flame and stars—
lots and lots of stars.

Which makes those crazy wise men even
crazier. Hey, let's follow that star that rose in
the east! The bright one. No, the other bright
one! Isn't it strange that one of them didn't say,
"Um, why are we doing this again?" or "Okay,

we can get there following the star, but how do we get back?"

Actually, I know the answer. I used to teach at a field camp in the Rocky Mountains. At night—especially a moonless night—you can see the entire firmament. You can see the edge of the Milky Way. You can see, it seems, forever, as if you are looking at heaven itself.

It's dark beneath a car. Without even the tiniest light, you could be turning something the wrong way. At Christmastime, even as the winter daylight fades and evening comes early, we have enough light to know which way to turn.

Lord, Christmas lights twinkle over our entire neighborhood. Let each be a star to guide wisdom into our homes. —Mark Collins

Digging Deeper: *John 1:14–17; 1 John 4:11*

A CHILD SHALL LEAD THEM

She bore a male Child who was to rule all nations
with a rod of iron. —Revelation 12:5 (NKJV)

When I was attending the University of Missouri, a Chinese man sat next to me in Educational Foundations class. He struggled to understand our language, so after class I would go over the notes with him. He was baffled by many of our customs and expressions.

One day he asked me, "What does it mean when you say, 'The hand that rocks the cradle rules the world'?"

I smiled. "Well, Chang, I think it means that if you take good care of babies, they may grow up to be presidents and kings, justices and queens."

"Ah," he lit up. "I like that. It is full of much wisdom."

I suppose there are other forms Jesus could have taken when He came to earth. How nice that He made His entry the same way all of us do, as a helpless baby.

"Christmas is for children," people say. Sometimes I forget how thrilling it is to them—the manger mystique, the charm of angels and wise men, "Jingle Bells" and candy, and opening presents with squeals of delight.

Sometimes I tire of Christmas, after celebrating sixty-three of them, but children do not. How I treat them may well determine the state of the world in fifty years. What a wonderful honor it is to rock the cradle and thereby rule the world.

Now I lay me down to sleep; I pray the Lord my soul to keep. —Daniel Schantz

Digging Deeper: *Luke 2:34–35; Psalm 127:3*

DECEMBER 13

HOLD THE BABY

Then took he him up in his arms, and blessed God,
and said, Lord, now lettest thou thy servant depart
in peace, according to thy word: For mine eyes
have seen thy salvation. —Luke 2:28—30 (KJV)

When I was a teenager during the turbulent six-
ties, my mother had a silver-haired friend named
Iva. Although Iva was the product of a more for-
mal generation, she didn't complain when our
church was invaded by an assortment of hippies
in faded jeans. Instead, Iva prayed, and one by
one this band of noisy young people made com-
mitments to Christ. I was one of them.

Then one Sunday, Iva's seat on the left side
of the sanctuary was empty. That morning Iva
had suffered a stroke and died instantly.

After the funeral, my mother told me, "Iva
somehow knew that she wouldn't live to see the
end result of the renewal we'd been praying for.

But she always smiled and said, 'It's all right. I've seen it start. I've held the baby.'"

Mom's statement puzzled me. It was only years later that I found out what "holding the baby" meant. When Mary and Joseph took baby Jesus to the temple, an old man named Simeon met them. Simeon had been promised that before he died he would see the Christ. An inner sense drew him to take the baby in his arms. In the face of a helpless infant, Simeon saw the King of kings.

Advent is about the hope we allow to flow through us as we, like Simeon, "hold the baby," knowing that from these wobbly beginnings will come greater, brighter, more wonderful things. Today, I've lived nearly as many decades as Iva. Thanks to the hope she had in my small beginnings of faith, I'd like to think that I've grown into someone like her.

Father, this Advent, keep my eyes open to the signs of Your work in my life, and give me the faith and patience to allow that work to grow. —Karen Barber

Digging Deeper: *Romans 5:5; Philippians 1:6*

DECEMBER 14

THE GREATEST GIFT

*"We observed his star at its rising, and have come
to pay him homage." —Matthew 2:2 (NRSV)*

Our Christmas tree was a big deal. Mom
whipped us into such a frenzy of waiting that
when the appointed day came for the tree, we were
beside ourselves. But what a day! Two Sundays
before Christmas, after church, Christmas
records were stacked on the record player and my
father would wrestle the tree into our house.

Then the lights—gazillions of lights! We
didn't touch them; Dad had to test them before
stringing them on the tree. Then he would
twine them deep inside the branches; Mom
didn't like to see the cords. Finally, Dad, breath-
ing relief, would retreat as the boxes were pulled
from the spare room where they'd waited since
Thanksgiving.

The big brown boxes were patched and ugly,

but what treasures they held: angels, stars, and miniature Nativities; homemade ornaments, store-bought ornaments, "Nana" ornaments my grandmother made, old ornaments from my mother's childhood; and some unclassifiable odds and ends. Mom, my sister Lori, and I would get to work, putting them up as music filled the house. Then we had garlands of some gold-colored stuff to drape on the branches.

The short December Sunday flew by. We waited, breathless, in the darkened house for my father to plug in the lights. When he did, though it didn't seem possible, our racing pulses slowed and we breathed deeply the light and warmth.

In that glow was peace, the antidote to the frenzy that had gripped us, a taste of what would come with Jesus.

Jesus, let me seek and find Your peace in all my Christmas busyness. —Marci Alborghetti

Digging Deeper: *Isaiah 9:6; Psalm 29:11*

December 15

Renewal

"Thus the saying 'One sows and another reaps'
is true. I sent you to reap what you have not
worked for." —John 4:37–38 (NIV)

The season of Advent corresponds to another
season in Pittsburgh: shoveling snow.

Fun fact about driving in Pittsburgh: if
you shovel out a parking space in front of your
house, you get to reserve that spot by placing an
object—usually a folding chair—in that space.
It doesn't have to be a chair; a garbage can or
an old sawhorse will do. (I've seen walkers and
vacuum cleaners serve as unofficial markers.)
While the object in the snow is there, no one but
you can park in the spot. Although this practice
exists in other northeastern cities, the tradition
is unofficially known as "the Pittsburgh parking
chair." Nice to be known for something.

Seems like a selfish gesture during the season

of gift giving, no? Right answer: no, it's not. Gifts are undeserved; a shoveled parking spot is earned. Technically speaking, parking chairs aren't legal, but local tradition dictates respect.

That's what makes Christmas gifts (and grace) so special: they're undeserved. Let's face it: we all deserve a little coal for our annual transgressions. Yet each Christmas we are forgiven and not because we've earned it. Can you think of a better birthday gift than renewal? So put a small chair in front of the crèche this year and reserve your spot. No one will take your place. No one can take your place.

Lord, You have invited all of us without reservation. This season, let us realize the chance for God and sinner to reconcile. —Mark Collins

Digging Deeper: *Ephesians 2:8—9*

DECEMBER 16

THE LIGHT OF
THE WORLD

> *"I am the light of the world: he that followeth
> me shall not walk in darkness, but shall
> have the light of life."* —John 8:12 *(KJV)*

A few years ago our family lived in Norway for
the month of June. Our most vivid memory is
the wondrous evening light. Until I experienced
it, I couldn't imagine the effect of living where
the sun never sets. It's difficult to describe the
energy and sense of well-being that constant
sunlight imparts.

No words can adequately depict the light of
our Savior. God's light is incomprehensible. After
talking with God, Moses's face shone so brightly
he had to cover it with a veil so the people would
be able to look at him. Christ comes to dispel my
darkness, my ultimate blindness: ignorance of
God's love and estrangement from my Creator.

On weekday mornings from September to May, I go to the kitchen and plug in a full-spectrum light box on the kitchen counter. Absorbing the brightness, I fill the coffeemaker, make breakfast, and pack lunches. This morning dose of light alleviates the seasonal depression I battle each winter. One morning recently, we all overslept, so my son grabbed a protein bar and we raced off to school; no time for the light box.

Once back home, as I went to my prayer corner, I brought the light box with me. Turning it on, I marveled at the beauty of the light illumining the cross on the wall. Then I knew: This time set apart for God to pray and read Scripture is my true light box, the way for His light to fill my soul. His light is greater than the darkness of winter, of lethargy or sadness or all my human foibles.

O Christ, the true light Who enlightens and sanctifies us, let the light of Your countenance be impressed upon us, that in it we may see Your unapproachable light.
—Mary Brown

Digging Deeper: *John 1:4–5; 1 John 1:5*

DECEMBER 17

A CHRISTMAS FOR THE HEART

And Mary said . . . be it unto me according
to thy word. —Luke 1:38 (KJV)

It was a sleepless night in 1955, and I lay awake with a deep and insistent longing for a child. Married just over a year, we were living in a tiny attic apartment we could barely afford. We'd decided to wait until we had some financial security before starting our family. Yet this longing felt insatiable. Unable to sleep, I got up, went to my prayer chair, opened my Bible to Luke 1 and reread the familiar story of Gabriel's announcement to Mary.

I pictured a small, open-windowed hut in Nazareth filled with a bright, unearthly light, and I overheard Mary's response to the archangel: "How shall this be?" I felt her doubt in my bones because I, too, was convinced of the impossibility of having a child at this time. Gabriel spoke again. "The Holy Ghost shall come upon thee, and the power of the Highest shall overshadow thee. . . . For with God nothing shall be impossible."

A puzzled look stole over the smooth young face. A breathless silence hung in the air. Then Mary lowered her head and with a serene smile responded, "Be it unto me according to thy word." To my own amazement and totally beyond reason, I found myself answering with her. *Be it unto me according to Thy word.*

That Christmas Eve, as we gathered with our extended family to open gifts, I was overjoyed to receive a layette, a dozen diapers, and a rattle, in anticipation of our first child who was due to be born six months later. Those gifts were precious, but I knew in my heart that the dearest gift was the one I held within me.

My childbearing years are long past, but I still carry a Holy Child within me. It is the Christ Child. I can sense His presence there whenever I touch my heart and whisper His name.

O Child of Light, pierce the dark within that I may know
Your presence. —Marilyn Morgan King

Digging Deeper: *Matthew 28:10; Hebrews 13:5*

....

DECEMBER 18

THE CROSS ABOVE
THE WORLD

"You are to go into all the world and preach the Good
News to everyone, everywhere." —Mark 16:15 *(TLB)*

My Christmas visit with my son Michael's family began like most.

But one morning after breakfast, the day took a different turn. We tuned up our singing voices and headed to join our "team" at a nearby care facility. All over town, members of Michael's church were doing the same thing. All during the Christmas season, pastors and laypeople visit every nursing and long-term care home in the city as part of their mission to share Christ's love.

About thirty residents were waiting. We sang "O Little Town of Bethlehem," "Joy to the World" and all five verses of "We Three Kings." Someone read the Christmas story. We gave candy and gifts—lovingly chosen and paid for by church members—to every resident. Then it was time for tea, cookies, and sharing.

One man had rows of military ribbons and medals pinned to his bathrobe. "I'll be rejoining my unit in England tomorrow," he told me. "The war's not won, you know." A woman in her seventies was worried about her ninety-plus-year-old mother: "I don't think she can cope if I go first." A young man receiving wound care was effusive in thanks for his gift of socks. Later, I learned it was the only package he would open and our group would be his only visitors.

As I closed my eyes for the prayer before we left, I pictured one particular ornament from the Chrismon tree at my church: the Cross of Christ on top of the world. I opened my eyes and looked at the residents, and I knew that this Christmas, we were where we were supposed to be, doing what the Lord of all called us to do.

Lord and lover of the world, let this day be the beginning of my own loving outreach. —Penney Schwab

Digging Deeper: *Hebrews 12:2*

....

DECEMBER 19

INTO ALL THE EARTH

Have they not heard? Yes verily, their sound went into all the earth, and their words unto the ends of the world. —Romans 10:18 *(KJV)*

By hovering near the Christmas tree for hours, I had become a master at recognizing those pesky presents by the time I was seven or eight.

As soon as I picked one up and gave it a little shake, I knew exactly what it was: an ornament. Back then I saw those neatly wrapped, lightweight boxes as necessary evils that I had to tear through and politely thank my grandmother Bebee for before I could get to the good stuff. Every year she gave ornaments to each of us grandkids. They came from her travels with my grandfather, and over time we'd received tree-hangers from all over the world. There was a wooden Great Wall from China, a tin Big Ben from London, and crudely carved mangers and stars from places I'd never heard of. On the back of each was the year and the place it came from, neatly written with a black marker.

All these years later those same ornaments have taken on a unique importance as my son, Harrison, and I decorate our tree. They remind me, of course, that I was always in my grandmother's heart as she traveled far and wide. But somehow they've also become symbols of the greatness of God, as they bear witness to the impact that Christ's birth has had on our world.

"Where is this one from, Daddy?" Harrison asks for the umpteenth time.

"That's a Taj Mahal from India," I reply, imagining the little shop in Agra that Bebee must have visited to find such a treasure.

"India?" Harrison replies with amazement. "I didn't know people that far away knew who Jesus is."

Isn't it wonderful to know they do?

Father, Your Spirit fills heaven and earth, and Your
Word truly reaches the ends of the world. —Brock Kidd

Digging Deeper: *Mark 16:15; Acts 1:8*

....

DECEMBER 20

A SAVIOR IN THE STRAW

Even the night shall be light about me.
—Psalm 139:11 (NKJV)

It's not how I would have done it. If I had news
as big as the gospel, I would have called simulta-
neous news conferences at high noon, in Athens
and Alexandria, in Jerusalem and Rome. But
when God announced the birth of His Son, He
did so at night, in a rural pasture. Jealous kings
and picky Pharisees were slumbering then, but
receptive shepherds were watching the sky when
it exploded with the glory of God.

Darkness is not my favorite time. Since
childhood I have needed a night-light to make it

to sunrise. I also own thirty-eight flashlights. It seems like everything gets worse at night: aches and pains, anxieties, regrets. At times I can't tell the difference between my nightmares and reality until my wife, Sharon, nudges me and asks, "Are you okay, hon?"

Yet, even I welcome darkness during the Christmas season. Without it, I could not enjoy the necklaces of light that grace the trees and homes of our neighborhood. Without darkness, I could not see the flickering candles of the carolers coming up our sidewalk. Without darkness, I couldn't enjoy our traditional candlelight Christmas supper.

Spiritual darkness can settle over a person at any season. Even at Christmas, things go wrong with marriage and health. Temptations sneak up on you, just when you're supposed to be singing "Joy to the World." At such times, it's good to step outdoors and look up at the stars. The night sky is filled with a trillion eyes, the eyes of angels, watching over us, longing to help us find our way back to the light.

Thank You, Father, for not leaving me in the dark.
—Daniel Schantz

Digging Deeper: *Psalm 27:1; Revelation 21:23*

....

DECEMBER 21

LA POSADA

*There was no room for them in
the inn. —Luke 2:7 (KJV)*

For fifteen years while we lived in Wyoming, our friends Dick and Julie Lefevre always invited us to their posada. This Mexican Christmas celebration combines caroling with a reenactment of Mary and Joseph seeking shelter that holy night in Bethlehem. Although few of us were Mexican, all of us enjoyed the tradition, which kept us close to the heart of Christmas.

Carolers, bundled in parkas and carrying lanterns, would trek to friends' homes and sing a plea to be let in so that Mary could rest. The "innkeeper," usually someone from our choir, would step outside and sing an unaccompanied refusal from his or her porch. When temperatures plunged below zero, the singer's breath hung in the air like smoke.

While the carolers sang traditional carols, the innkeeper would quickly pack up his or her family and Mexican food to share, then join the procession to the next inn. After three or four stops, the carolers, now stamping feet to keep warm, wound up at the Lefevres'. These gracious innkeepers sang, "Yes! Come in!" to the chilled singers, who duly trooped past flickering candles into their home. The fiesta had begun.

For the next several hours we savored a groaning board of Mexican fare, including huge pans of enchiladas and a Christmas salad with beets. When the older kids left to ice skate, the younger ones whacked the piñata. Then someone would start strumming a guitar. We'd sit on the floor and sing Christmas songs until, with a start, we realized that the ice rink had closed and we dashed to fetch our youngsters.

While I lived in Wyoming, we rarely

celebrated Christmas with our relatives from the East Coast. But my posada family always made me feel at home in this ritual of food and song.

There was always room in the inn.

Divine Comforter, help us to remember that when we welcome others, we welcome You. —Gail Thorell Schilling

Digging Deeper: *Hebrews 13:2*

....

DECEMBER 22

FEAR NOT

Behold, the angel of the Lord appeared unto him in a dream, saying, Joseph, thou son of David, fear not to take unto thee Mary thy wife. —Matthew 1:20 *(KJV)*

Carol was six months pregnant with our first child that December, the year we saw Advent through new eyes.

When I sat in the pew and heard Bible lessons about waiting, I wondered what our child would be like. What sort of gifts would he have? Who would he take after in our family? As an expectant father I had my own set of worries: Would I be able to make enough to support a child? Would I be patient enough as a father? What if I had a kid who wanted to play catch every night? I was terrible at baseball.

After the service people would smile at Carol and say to me, "Aren't you excited about having a baby?" Scared to death was more like it. Then, one Sunday, the lesson was about Joseph and how he was ready to walk away from Mary when he discovered she was pregnant, until an angel in a dream reassured him, "Fear not." The rest he had to take on trust. The trip to Bethlehem, the visits from wise men and shepherds, the hurried escape to Egypt—the Christmas story wouldn't have happened if Joseph hadn't trusted God.

So I promised I would trust God.

When William was born, I managed to find the energy to get up in the middle of the night when I had to, and in those first few years of parenthood we were always able to pay the bills. When he grew old enough to want to throw a ball after school, I learned how to throw one too. Now as he enters his fourteenth year, I confess I have a whole new set of worries. What if he falls in with the wrong set of kids in high school? What if I can't afford college? What if he does poorly on his entrance exams?

Then I remember: "Fear not." It's a gift I could use every Advent.

Thank You, God, for the gift of faith. —Rick Hamlin

Digging Deeper: *Mark 11:24; Isaiah 41:10*

....

DECEMBER 23

GOOD NEWS OF GREAT JOY

"Come, follow me," Jesus said. —Matthew 4:19 (NIV)

The word *follow* doesn't actually appear in the Christmas story, but it's a familiar part of it. The wise men followed the star to the manger in Bethlehem. We don't know exactly who they were, but clearly they had studied the stars and had confidence that the one they followed would lead them to the birthplace of a king. Then, in a dream, they were warned not to return to King Herod to tell him what they had found and they followed that advice. They understood that what and whom they followed was very important.

I learned that same lesson in a vivid way a few weeks ago. I was part of a caravan traveling to Sedona, Arizona, for a women's retreat. I began following the line of cars from the church parking lot, and as we spread out on I-17, I picked a white SUV to follow and settled in for the two-hour drive. About an hour later, the SUV put on its turn signal and exited the freeway. I followed, although I knew we weren't close to our exit. Then I realized I'd been following the wrong car! Fortunately, I knew the way to Sedona and got back on the right road.

From faith to politics to diets, we're constantly bombarded with messages about what and whom to follow. But over and over in the Gospels, Jesus has one message: "Follow Me."

As Advent nears an end and I approach the celebration of Christ's birth, the obvious question is "Where do I go from here?" Jesus provides the answer in two simple words: "Follow Me."

Dear Jesus, help me keep my Christmas promise to follow You in my thoughts, words, and actions, not just at this special time of year, but all the time.
—Gina Bridgeman

Digging Deeper: *John 10:27; Galatians 5:25*

....

DECEMBER 24

IMAGE OF PRAISE

"My soul magnifies the Lord." —Luke 1:46 (NRSV)

I didn't know it was to be, after fourteen years, my last Christmas Eve in Alaska. Yet had I known, I wouldn't have changed a thing.

After a wonderful dinner with friends at their alpaca farm, I slipped outdoors in the chilly night air to spend time alone with God under the stars—and to enjoy the woolly animals quietly bedded down in their lean-to shelter near the house. The earthy aroma of hay filled my nose. More than a dozen alpacas followed me curiously with their intelligent big brown eyes. They weren't the traditional ox and donkey, but the scent and feel of the scene transported me to that first Bethlehem Christmas Eve.

All at once I began to softly sing "Away in a Manger" to the animals. This roused the inquisitive rooster, who fluttered out from his crumpled bed of straw beneath the deck. He strutted about, pecking at bits of hay in the snow. My song ended, but I couldn't stop praising God.

I looked up at the stars and called out, "Glory to God! Peace on earth! Christ is born!" Suddenly the rooster stopped his pecking and crowed three times, as if he were repeating my praise. We kept it up for several minutes, until I was bursting with such laughter and rejoicing that I ran inside to share it with everyone.

Was there, I wonder, a rooster in the hay the night Jesus was born? If there was, did he let out a zesty crow at the young Savior's first cry? It's something I'd like to ask Mary. Somehow, I don't think she would find my question strange at all.

Jesus, You are so glorious that all creation sings Your praise!
—Carol Knapp

Digging Deeper: *Psalms 19:1; 145:3*

....

DECEMBER 25

A TIME FOR GIVING

The shepherds returned, glorifying and praising God for all the things they had heard and seen. —Luke 2:20 *(NIV)*

There comes that time on Christmas Day when all the gifts are given, brunch is consumed, the guests have left and there is nothing more to unwrap. In my family we go to our little stockpile of presents and take a mental inventory.

Who was it that gave me that nice blue sweater? That tie will go well with my brown suit. I must tell my parents that the towels are perfect. The boys inspect their books while Carol fantasizes about a recipe in her new cookbook. Then as I put on the CD I was given, Timothy looks up from his new board game. "Dad, do you want to play Risk?" he asks.

"Sure," I say. William joins us for the game, as Carol settles in with the novel that her sister sent. We roll the dice and are soon absorbed in strategizing over the territory on the Risk board. As I listen to the music and hear Carol turn pages in her book (and listen to Timothy agonize over how to conquer Asia), I think about how grateful I am to have this family, to have this apartment for a home, to have friends and family who care enough about me to send gifts.

It's not the presents that have made this a fine Christmas Day. It's this time together, lounging on a winter's afternoon. It's being able to savor it without having to rush to the office or read my e-mail. It's hearing Carol chuckle in the armchair and watching the boys beat their dear old dad. Sure enough, busyness will return, but this day has reminded me of all the things I have that can't be wrapped up. That feels like my holiday gift. And for that I thank the good Lord.

Dear God, let me savor every day as though it were Christmas. —Rick Hamlin

Digging Deeper: *Deuteronomy 26:11; James 1:17*

BIBLE TRANSLATIONS

Scripture quotations marked (KJV) are taken from the *King James Version*. Public domain.

Scripture quotations marked (NIV) are taken from the *Holy Bible, New International Version*®, NIV®. Copyright © 1973, 1978, 1984, 2011 by Biblica, Inc.® Used by permission of Zondervan. All rights reserved worldwide. www.Zondervan.com. The "NIV" and "New International Version" are trademarks registered in the United States Patent and Trademark Office by Biblica, Inc.®

Scripture quotations marked (NKJV) are taken from the *New King James Version*®. © 1982 by Thomas Nelson. Used by permission. All rights reserved.

Scripture quotations marked (NLT) are taken from the *Holy Bible, New Living Translation*. © 1996, 2004, 2007, 2013 by Tyndale House Foundation. Used by permission of Tyndale House Publishers, Inc., Carol Stream, Illinois 60188. All rights reserved.

Scripture quotations marked (NRSV) are taken from the *New Revised Standard Version Bible*. Copyright © 1989 National Council of the Churches of Christ in the United States of America. Used by permission. All rights reserved.

Scripture quotations marked (TLB) are taken from *The Living Bible*. Copyright © 1971 by Tyndale House Publishers, Inc., Wheaton, Illinois 60188. All rights reserved.

Especially for You

Join us for

New Year, New You—

7 Resolutions That Matter Most

Guideposts.org/NewYear

DAILY
GUIDEPOSTS

A community of *friends* that accompanies
you on a path to a greater *connection*
with God, lifts your *spirits*, and reminds
you of all that is *precious* in life . . .
every day of the year.

 DailyGuideposts   DailyGuideposts

Daily Guideposts 2017

A Spirit-Lifting Devotional

Daily Guideposts 2017 centers on the theme "In God's Hands" from Isaiah 41:10 and is filled with brand-new devotions from forty-nine writers. Readers will enjoy a Scripture verse; a true first-person story told in a conversational style, which shares the ways God speaks in the ordinary events of life; and a brief prayer to help focus readers to apply the message. "Digging Deeper" provides additional Bible references that relate to the reading.

In just five minutes a day, *Daily Guideposts 2017* helps readers find the spiritual richness in their own lives and welcomes them into a remarkable family of more than one million people brought together by a desire to grow spiritually every day of the year.

Guideposts

New York

Mornings with Jesus 2017

Daily Encouragement for Your Soul

> *"Come to me, all you who are weary and burdened, and I will give you rest."*
> —Matthew 11:28 NIV

We hear Jesus's words and want to respond, but so often we feel we're too busy, too anxious, or too heavily burdened to take hold of His invitation. *Mornings with Jesus 2017*, an annual, 365-day devotional, is your entry into His world. Jesus will comfort you, and you'll experience the delight and challenge of knowing Him and living for Him.

In *Mornings with Jesus 2017*, you can read and reflect on one devotion each day that will encourage you to embrace Jesus's love, to lay down your worries and walk with Him, and to focus on Him as Redeemer, Friend, and Faithful One. Every day, you will enjoy a Scripture verse, a reflection on Jesus's words, and a faith step that inspires and challenges you in your daily walk of living a Christlike life.

Daily Guideposts is published by Guideposts, a remarkable family of readers and writers who share true stories of hope and inspiration and home to OurPrayer ministry. You can get free e-books and e-newsletters at Guideposts.org and request prayers at OurPrayer.org.

Daily Guideposts

Celebrating over forty years of
spirit-lifting devotions!

CHAPTER 1

Introduction

Most honourable Theophilus:
Many people have written accounts about the events that took place* among us. ²They used as their source material the reports circulating among us from the early disciples and other eyewitnesses of what God has done in fulfilment of his promises. ³Having carefully investigated all of these accounts from the beginning, I have decided to write a careful summary for you, ⁴to reassure you of the truth of all you were taught.

The Birth of John the Baptist Foretold

⁵It all begins with a Jewish priest, Zechariah, who lived when Herod was king of Judea. Zechariah was a member of the priestly order of Abijah. His wife, Elizabeth, was also from the priestly line of Aaron. ⁶Zechariah and Elizabeth were righteous in God's eyes, careful to obey all of the Lord's commandments and regulations. ⁷They had no children because Elizabeth was barren, and now they were both very old.

⁸One day Zechariah was serving God in the Temple, for his order was on duty that week. ⁹As was the custom of the priests, he was chosen by lot to enter the sanctuary and burn incense in the Lord's presence. ¹⁰While the incense was being burned, a great crowd stood outside, praying.

¹¹Zechariah was in the sanctuary when an angel of the Lord appeared, standing to the right of the incense altar. ¹²Zechariah was overwhelmed with fear. ¹³But the angel

1

said, "Don't be afraid, Zechariah! For God has heard your prayer, and your wife, Elizabeth, will bear you a son! And you are to name him John. ¹⁴You will have great joy and gladness, and many will rejoice with you at his birth, ¹⁵for he will be great in the eyes of the Lord. He must never touch wine or strong drink, and he will be filled with the Holy Spirit, even before his birth.* ¹⁶And he will persuade many Israelites to turn to the Lord their God. ¹⁷He will be a man with the spirit and power of Elijah, the prophet of old. He will precede the coming of the Lord, preparing the people for his arrival. He will turn the hearts of the fathers to their children, and he will change disobedient minds to accept godly wisdom."*

¹⁸Zechariah said to the angel, "How can I know this will happen? I'm an old man now, and my wife is also getting on in years."

¹⁹Then the angel said, "I am Gabriel! I stand in the very presence of God. It was he who sent me to bring you this good news! ²⁰And now, since you didn't believe what I said, you won't be able to speak until the child is born. For my words will certainly come true at the proper time."

²¹Meanwhile, the people were waiting for Zechariah to come out, wondering why he was taking so long. ²²When he finally did come out, he couldn't speak to them. Then they realized from his gestures that he must have seen a vision in the Temple sanctuary.

²³He stayed at the Temple until his term of service was over, and then he returned home. ²⁴Soon afterwards his wife, Elizabeth, became pregnant and went into seclusion for five months. ²⁵"How kind the Lord is!" she exclaimed. "He has taken away my disgrace of having no children!"

ISBN 0 – 9015.1848 – 4   2005/20M

Published by: The Scottish Bible Society, 7 Hampton Terrace, Edinburgh, EH12 5XU

Typesetting copyright © The Scottish Bible Society.

Typeset in Souvenir BQ by Solidus www.solid-us.com

Printed in Italy by Lego s.p.a.

Luke

Tells the Good News

A quick look at this book

The Birth of Jesus Foretold

²⁶ In the sixth month of Elizabeth's pregnancy, God sent the angel Gabriel to Nazareth, a village in Galilee, ²⁷ to a virgin named Mary. She was engaged to be married to a man named Joseph, a descendant of King David. ²⁸ Gabriel appeared to her and said, "Greetings, favoured woman! The Lord is with you!'"

²⁹ Confused and disturbed, Mary tried to think what the angel could mean. ³⁰ "Don't be frightened, Mary," the angel told her, "for God has decided to bless you! ³¹ You will become pregnant and have a son, and you are to name him Jesus. ³² He will be very great and will be called the Son of the Most High. And the Lord God will give him the throne of his ancestor David. ³³ And he will reign over Israel* for ever; his Kingdom will never end!"

³⁴ Mary asked the angel, "But how can I have a baby? I am a virgin."

³⁵ The angel replied, "The Holy Spirit will come upon you, and the power of the Most High will overshadow you. So the baby born to you will be holy, and he will be called the Son of God. ³⁶ What's more, your relative Elizabeth has become pregnant in her old age! People used to say she was barren, but she's already in her sixth month. ³⁷ For nothing is impossible with God."

³⁸ Mary responded, "I am the Lord's servant, and I am willing to accept whatever he wants. May everything you have said come true." And then the angel left.

Mary Visits Elizabeth

³⁹ A few days later Mary hurried to the hill country of Judea, to the town ⁴⁰ where Zechariah lived. She entered

the house and greeted Elizabeth. ⁴¹ At the sound of Mary's greeting, Elizabeth's child leaped within her, and Elizabeth was filled with the Holy Spirit.

⁴² Elizabeth gave a glad cry and exclaimed to Mary, "You are blessed by God above all other women, and your child is blessed. ⁴³ What an honour this is, that the mother of my Lord should visit me! ⁴⁴ When you came in and greeted me, my baby jumped for joy the instant I heard your voice! ⁴⁵ You are blessed, because you believed that the Lord would do what he said."

The Magnificat: Mary's Song of Praise

⁴⁶ Mary responded,
"Oh, how I praise the Lord.
⁴⁷   How I rejoice in God my Saviour!
⁴⁸ For he took notice of his lowly servant girl,
and now generation after generation
will call me blessed.
⁴⁹ For he, the Mighty One, is holy,
and he has done great things for me.
⁵⁰ His mercy goes on from generation to generation,
to all who fear him.
⁵¹ His mighty arm does tremendous things!
How he scatters the proud and haughty ones!
⁵² He has taken princes from their thrones
and exalted the lowly.
⁵³ He has satisfied the hungry with good things
and sent the rich away with empty hands.
⁵⁴ And how he has helped his servant Israel!
He has not forgotten his promise to be merciful.
⁵⁵ For he promised our ancestors—Abraham and his
children—

to be merciful to them for ever."

[56] Mary stayed with Elizabeth about three months and then went back to her own home.

The Birth of John the Baptist

[57] Now it was time for Elizabeth's baby to be born, and it was a boy. [58] The word spread quickly to her neighbours and relatives that the Lord had been very kind to her, and everyone rejoiced with her.

[59] When the baby was eight days old, all the relatives and friends came for the circumcision ceremony. They wanted to name him Zechariah, after his father. [60] But Elizabeth said, "No! His name is John!"

[61] "What?" they exclaimed. "There is no one in all your family by that name." [62] So they asked the baby's father, communicating to him by making gestures. [63] He motioned for a writing tablet, and to everyone's surprise he wrote, "His name is John!" [64] Instantly Zechariah could speak again, and he began praising God.

[65] Wonder fell upon the whole neighbourhood, and the news of what had happened spread throughout the Judean hills. [66] Everyone who heard about it reflected on these events and asked, "I wonder what this child will turn out to be? For the hand of the Lord is surely upon him in a special way."

Zechariah's Prophecy

[67] Then his father, Zechariah, was filled with the Holy Spirit and gave this prophecy:
[68] "Praise the Lord, the God of Israel,
   because he has visited his people and redeemed them.

⁶⁹ He has sent us a mighty Saviour
    from the royal line of his servant David,
⁷⁰ just as he promised
    through his holy prophets long ago.
⁷¹ Now we will be saved from our enemies
    and from all who hate us.
⁷² He has been merciful to our ancestors
    by remembering his sacred covenant with them,
⁷³   the covenant he gave to our ancestor Abraham.
⁷⁴ We have been rescued from our enemies,
    so we can serve God without fear,
⁷⁵   in holiness and righteousness for ever.
⁷⁶ "And you, my little son,
    will be called the prophet of the Most High,
    because you will prepare the way for the Lord.
⁷⁷ You will tell his people how to find salvation
    through forgiveness of their sins.
⁷⁸ Because of God's tender mercy,
    the light from heaven is about to break upon us,
⁷⁹ to give light to those who sit in darkness and in the
        shadow of death,
    and to guide us to the path of peace."
⁸⁰ John grew up and became strong in spirit. Then he
lived out in the wilderness until he began his public
ministry to Israel.

CHAPTER 2

The Birth of Jesus

At that time the Roman emperor, Augustus, decreed that a census should be taken throughout the Roman Empire. ²(This was the first census taken when Quirinius was governor of Syria.) ³All returned to their own towns to register for this census. ⁴And because Joseph was a descendant of King David, he had to go to Bethlehem in Judea, David's ancient home. He travelled there from the village of Nazareth in Galilee. ⁵He took with him Mary, his fiancé, who was obviously pregnant by this time.

⁶And while they were there, the time came for her baby to be born. ⁷She gave birth to her first child, a son. She wrapped him snugly in strips of cloth and laid him in a manger, because there was no room for them in the village inn.

The Shepherds and Angels

⁸That night some shepherds were in the fields outside the village, guarding their flocks of sheep. ⁹Suddenly, an angel of the Lord appeared among them, and the radiance of the Lord's glory surrounded them. They were terribly frightened, ¹⁰but the angel reassured them. "Don't be afraid!" he said. "I bring you good news of great joy for everyone! ¹¹The Saviour—yes, the Messiah, the Lord—has been born tonight in Bethlehem, the city of David! ¹²And this is how you will recognize him: You will find a baby lying in a manger, wrapped snugly in strips of cloth!"

¹³ Suddenly, the angel was joined by a vast host of others—the armies of heaven—praising God:
¹⁴ "Glory to God in the highest heaven,
and peace on earth to all whom God favours."'
¹⁵ When the angels had returned to heaven, the shepherds said to each other, "Come on, let's go to Bethlehem! Let's see this wonderful thing that has happened, which the Lord has told us about."

¹⁶ They ran to the village and found Mary and Joseph. And there was the baby, lying in the manger. ¹⁷ Then the shepherds told everyone what had happened and what the angel had said to them about this child. ¹⁸ All who heard the shepherds' story were astonished, ¹⁹ but Mary quietly treasured these things in her heart and thought about them often. ²⁰ The shepherds went back to their fields and flocks, glorifying and praising God for what the angels had told them, and because they had seen the child, just as the angel had said.

Jesus is Presented in the Temple

²¹ Eight days later, when the baby was circumcised, he was named Jesus, the name given him by the angel even before he was conceived.

²² Then it was time for the purification offering, as required by the law of Moses after the birth of a child; so his parents took him to Jerusalem to present him to the Lord. ²³ The law of the Lord says, "If a woman's first child is a boy, he must be dedicated to the Lord."* ²⁴ So they offered a sacrifice according to what was required in the law of the Lord—"either a pair of turtle-doves or two young pigeons."*

8

The Prophecy of Simeon

[25] Now there was a man named Simeon who lived in Jerusalem. He was a righteous man and very devout. He was filled with the Holy Spirit, and he eagerly expected the Messiah to come and rescue Israel. [26] The Holy Spirit had revealed to him that he would not die until he had seen the Lord's Messiah. [27] That day the Spirit led him to the Temple. So when Mary and Joseph came to present the baby Jesus to the Lord as the law required, [28] Simeon was there. He took the child in his arms and praised God, saying,

[29] "Lord, now I can die in peace!
　　As you promised me,
[30] I have seen the Saviour
[31] you have given to all people.
[32] He is a light to reveal God to the nations,
　　and he is the glory of your people Israel!"

[33] Joseph and Mary were amazed at what was being said about Jesus. [34] Then Simeon blessed them, and he said to Mary, "This child will be rejected by many in Israel, and it will be their undoing. But he will be the greatest joy to many others. [35] Thus, the deepest thoughts of many hearts will be revealed. And a sword will pierce your very soul."

The Prophecy of Anna

[36] Anna, a prophet, was also there in the Temple. She was the daughter of Phanuel, of the tribe of Asher, and was very old. She was a widow, for her husband had died when they had been married only seven years. [37] She was now eighty-four years old. She never left the Temple but stayed there day and night, worshipping God with fasting

and prayer. ³⁸She came along just as Simeon was talking with Mary and Joseph, and she began praising God. She talked about Jesus to everyone who had been waiting for the promised King to come and deliver Jerusalem.

³⁹When Jesus' parents had fulfilled all the requirements of the law of the Lord, they returned home to Nazareth in Galilee. ⁴⁰There the child grew up healthy and strong. He was filled with wisdom beyond his years, and God placed his special favour upon him.

Jesus Speaks with the Teachers

⁴¹Every year Jesus' parents went to Jerusalem for the Passover festival. ⁴²When Jesus was twelve years old, they attended the festival as usual. ⁴³After the celebration was over, they started home to Nazareth, but Jesus stayed behind in Jerusalem. His parents didn't miss him at first, ⁴⁴because they assumed he was with friends among the other travellers. But when he didn't show up that evening, they started to look for him among their relatives and friends. ⁴⁵When they couldn't find him, they went back to Jerusalem to search for him there. ⁴⁶Three days later they finally discovered him. He was in the Temple, sitting among the religious teachers, discussing deep questions with them. ⁴⁷And all who heard him were amazed at his understanding and his answers.

⁴⁸His parents didn't know what to think. "Son!" his mother said to him. "Why have you done this to us? Your father and I have been frantic, searching for you everywhere."

⁴⁹"But why did you need to search?" he asked. "You should have known that I would be in my Father's house."* ⁵⁰But they didn't understand what he meant.

⁵¹ Then he returned to Nazareth with them and was obedient to them; and his mother stored all these things in her heart. ⁵² So Jesus grew both in height and in wisdom, and he was loved by God and by all who knew him.

CHAPTER 3

John the Baptist Prepares the Way

It was now the fifteenth year of the reign of Tiberius, the Roman emperor. Pilate was governor over Judea*ª; Herod Antipas was ruler*ᵇ over Galilee; his brother Philip was ruler*ᶜ over Iturea and Traconitis; Lysanias was ruler over Abilene. ² Annas and Caiaphas were the high priests. At this time a message from God came to John son of Zechariah, who was living out in the wilderness. ³ Then John went from place to place on both sides of the River Jordan, preaching that people should be baptized to show that they had turned from their sins and turned to God to be forgiven.* ⁴ Isaiah had spoken of John when he said,

"He is a voice shouting in the wilderness:
'Prepare a pathway for the Lord's coming!
    Make a straight road for him!
⁵ Fill in the valleys,
    and level the mountains and hills!
Straighten the curves,
    and smooth out the rough places!
⁶ And then all people will see
    the salvation sent from God.'"*

⁷ Here is a sample of John's preaching to the crowds that came for baptism: "You brood of snakes! Who warned you to flee God's coming judgement? ⁸ Prove by the way you live that you have really turned from your sins and turned to God. Don't just say, 'We're safe—we're the descendants of Abraham.' That proves nothing. God can change these stones here into children of Abraham. ⁹ Even now the axe of God's judgement is poised, ready to sever your roots. Yes, every tree that does not produce good fruit will be chopped down and thrown into the fire."

¹⁰ The crowd asked, "What should we do?"

¹¹ John replied, "If you have two coats, give one to the poor. If you have food, share it with those who are hungry."

¹² Even corrupt tax collectors came to be baptized and asked, "Teacher, what should we do?"

¹³ "Show your honesty," he replied. "Make sure you collect no more taxes than the Roman government requires you to."

¹⁴ "What should we do?" asked some soldiers.

John replied, "Don't extort money, and don't accuse people of things you know they didn't do. And be content with your pay."

¹⁵ Everyone was expecting the Messiah to come soon, and they were eager to know whether John might be the Messiah. ¹⁶ John answered their questions by saying, "I baptize with* water; but someone is coming soon who is greater than I am—so much greater that I am not even worthy to be his slave.* He will baptize you with the Holy Spirit and with fire.* ¹⁷ He is ready to separate the chaff from the grain with his winnowing fork. Then he will clean up the threshing area, storing the grain in his

barn but burning the chaff with never-ending fire." [18] John used many such warnings as he announced the Good News to the people.

[19] John also publicly criticized Herod Antipas, ruler of Galilee, for marrying Herodias, his brother's wife, and for many other wrongs he had done. [20] So Herod put John in prison, adding this sin to his many others.

The Baptism of Jesus

[21] One day when the crowds were being baptized, Jesus himself was baptized. As he was praying, the heavens opened, [22] and the Holy Spirit descended on him in the form of a dove. And a voice from heaven said, "You are my beloved Son, and I am fully pleased with you.*"

The Record of Jesus' Ancestors

[23] Jesus was about thirty years old when he began his public ministry.

Jesus was known as the son of Joseph.

Joseph was the son of Heli.
[24] Heli was the son of Matthat.
Matthat was the son of Levi.
Levi was the son of Melki.
Melki was the son of Jannai.
Jannai was the son of Joseph.
[25] Joseph was the son of Mattathias.
Mattathias was the son of Amos.
Amos was the son of Nahum.
Nahum was the son of Esli.
Esli was the son of Naggai.
[26] Naggai was the son of Maath.

Maath was the son of Mattathias.
Mattathias was the son of Semein.
Semein was the son of Josech.
Josech was the son of Joda.
²⁷ Joda was the son of Joanan.
Joanan was the son of Rhesa.
Rhesa was the son of Zerubbabel.
Zerubbabel was the son of Shealtiel.
Shealtiel was the son of Neri.
²⁸ Neri was the son of Melki.
Melki was the son of Addi.
Addi was the son of Cosam.
Cosam was the son of Elmadam.
Elmadam was the son of Er.
²⁹ Er was the son of Joshua.
Joshua was the son of Eliezer.
Eliezer was the son of Jorim.
Jorim was the son of Matthat.
Matthat was the son of Levi.
³⁰ Levi was the son of Simeon.
Simeon was the son of Judah.
Judah was the son of Joseph.
Joseph was the son of Jonam.
Jonam was the son of Eliakim.
³¹ Eliakim was the son of Melea.
Melea was the son of Menna.
Menna was the son of Mattatha.
Mattatha was the son of Nathan.
Nathan was the son of David.
³² David was the son of Jesse.
Jesse was the son of Obed.
Obed was the son of Boaz.

Boaz was the son of Salmon.*
Salmon was the son of Nahshon.
³³Nahshon was the son of Amminadab.
Amminadab was the son of Admin.
Admin was the son of Arni.*
Arni was the son of Hezron.
Hezron was the son of Perez.
Perez was the son of Judah.
³⁴Judah was the son of Jacob.
Jacob was the son of Isaac.
Isaac was the son of Abraham.
Abraham was the son of Terah.
Terah was the son of Nahor.
³⁵Nahor was the son of Serug.
Serug was the son of Reu.
Reu was the son of Peleg.
Peleg was the son of Eber.
Eber was the son of Shelah.
³⁶Shelah was the son of Cainan.
Cainan was the son of Arphaxad.
Arphaxad was the son of Shem.
Shem was the son of Noah.
Noah was the son of Lamech.
³⁷Lamech was the son of Methuselah.
Methuselah was the son of Enoch.
Enoch was the son of Jared.
Jared was the son of Mahalalel.
Mahalalel was the son of Kenan.
³⁸Kenan was the son of Enosh.*
Enosh was the son of Seth.
Seth was the son of Adam.
Adam was the son of God.

CHAPTER 4

The Temptation of Jesus

Then Jesus, full of the Holy Spirit, left the River Jordan. He was led by the Spirit to go out into the wilderness, ²where the Devil tempted him for forty days. He ate nothing all that time and was very hungry.

³Then the Devil said to him, "If you are the Son of God, change this stone into a loaf of bread."

⁴But Jesus told him, "No! The Scriptures say, 'People need more than bread for their life.'* "

⁵Then the Devil took him up and revealed to him all the kingdoms of the world in a moment of time. ⁶The Devil told him, "I will give you the glory of these kingdoms and authority over them—because they are mine to give to anyone I please. ⁷I will give it all to you if you will bow down and worship me."

⁸Jesus replied, "The Scriptures say,

'You must worship the Lord your God;
    serve only him.'* "

⁹Then the Devil took him to Jerusalem, to the highest point of the Temple, and said, "If you are the Son of God, jump off! ¹⁰For the Scriptures say,

'He orders his angels to protect and guard you.
¹¹And they will hold you with their hands
    to keep you from striking your foot on a stone.'* "

¹²Jesus responded, "The Scriptures also say, 'Do not test the Lord your God.'* "

¹³When the Devil had finished tempting Jesus, he left him until the next opportunity came.

Jesus Rejected at Nazareth

[14] Then Jesus returned to Galilee, filled with the Holy Spirit's power. Soon he became well known throughout the surrounding country. [15] He taught in their synagogues and was praised by everyone.

[16] When he came to the village of Nazareth, his boyhood home, he went as usual to the synagogue on the Sabbath and stood up to read the Scriptures. [17] The scroll containing the messages of Isaiah the prophet was handed to him, and he unrolled the scroll to the place where it says:

[18] "The Spirit of the Lord is upon me,
> for he has appointed me to preach Good News to
>   the poor.
He has sent me to proclaim
> that captives will be released,
> that the blind will see,
> that the downtrodden will be freed from their
>   oppressors,

[19] and that the time of the Lord's favour has come.*"

[20] He rolled up the scroll, handed it back to the attendant, and sat down. Everyone in the synagogue stared at him intently. [21] Then he said, "This Scripture has come true today before your very eyes!"

[22] All who were there spoke well of him and were amazed by the gracious words that fell from his lips. "How can this be?" they asked. "Isn't this Joseph's son?"

[23] Then he said, "Probably you will quote me that proverb, 'Physician, heal yourself'—meaning, 'Why don't you do miracles here in your home town like those you did in Capernaum?' [24] But the truth is, no prophet is accepted in his own home town.

²⁵ "Certainly there were many widows in Israel who needed help in Elijah's time, when there was no rain for three and a half years and hunger stalked the land. ²⁶ Yet Elijah was not sent to any of them. He was sent instead to a widow of Zarephath—a foreigner in the land of Sidon. ²⁷ Or think of the prophet Elisha, who healed Naaman, a Syrian, rather than the many lepers in Israel who needed help."

²⁸ When they heard this, the people in the synagogue were furious. ²⁹ Jumping up, they mobbed him and took him to the edge of the hill on which the city was built. They intended to push him over the cliff, ³⁰ but he slipped away through the crowd and left them.

Jesus Casts Out a Demon

³¹ Then Jesus went to Capernaum, a town in Galilee, and taught there in the synagogue every Sabbath day. ³² There, too, the people were amazed at the things he said, because he spoke with authority.

³³ Once when he was in the synagogue, a man possessed by a demon began shouting at Jesus, ³⁴ "Go away! Why are you bothering us, Jesus of Nazareth? Have you come to destroy us? I know who you are—the Holy One sent from God."

³⁵ Jesus cut him short. "Be silent!" he told the demon. "Come out of the man!" The demon threw the man to the floor as the crowd watched; then it left him without hurting him further.

³⁶ Amazed, the people exclaimed, "What authority and power this man's words possess! Even evil spirits obey him and flee at his command!" ³⁷ The story of what he had done spread like wildfire throughout the whole region.

Jesus Heals Many People

³⁸ After leaving the synagogue that day, Jesus went to Simon's home, where he found Simon's mother-in-law very sick with a high fever. "Please heal her," everyone begged. ³⁹ Standing at her bedside, he spoke to the fever, rebuking it, and immediately her temperature returned to normal. She got up at once and prepared a meal for them.

⁴⁰ As the sun went down that evening, people throughout the village brought sick family members to Jesus. No matter what their diseases were, the touch of his hand healed every one. ⁴¹ Some were possessed by demons; and the demons came out at his command, shouting, "You are the Son of God." But because they knew he was the Messiah, he stopped them and told them to be silent.

Jesus Continues to Preach

⁴² Early the next morning Jesus went out into the wilderness. The crowds searched everywhere for him, and when they finally found him, they begged him not to leave them. ⁴³ But he replied, "I must preach the Good News of the Kingdom of God in other places, too, because that is why I was sent." ⁴⁴ So he continued to travel around, preaching in synagogues throughout Judea.*

CHAPTER 5

The First Disciples

One day as Jesus was preaching on the shore of the Sea of Galilee,* great crowds pressed in on him to listen to the word of God. ²He noticed two empty boats at the water's edge, for the fishermen had left them and were washing their nets. ³Stepping into one of the boats, Jesus asked Simon,* its owner, to push it out into the water. So he sat in the boat and taught the crowds from there.

⁴When he had finished speaking, he said to Simon, "Now go out where it is deeper and let down your nets, and you will catch many fish."

⁵"Master," Simon replied, "we worked hard all last night and didn't catch a thing. But if you say so, we'll try again." ⁶And this time their nets were so full they began to tear! ⁷A shout for help brought their partners in the other boat, and soon both boats were filled with fish and on the verge of sinking.

⁸When Simon Peter realized what had happened, he fell to his knees before Jesus and said, "Oh, Lord, please leave me—I'm too much of a sinner to be around you." ⁹For he was awestruck by the size of their catch, as were the others with him. ¹⁰His partners, James and John, the sons of Zebedee, were also amazed.

Jesus replied to Simon, "Don't be afraid! From now on you'll be fishing for people!" ¹¹And as soon as they landed, they left everything and followed Jesus.

Jesus Heals a Man with Leprosy

¹²In one of the villages, Jesus met a man with an advanced case of leprosy. When the man saw Jesus, he fell to the ground, face down in the dust, begging to be healed. "Lord," he said, "if you want to, you can make me well again."

¹³Jesus reached out and touched the man. "I want to," he said. "Be healed!" And instantly the leprosy disappeared. ¹⁴Then Jesus instructed him not to tell

anyone what had happened. He said, "Go straight to the priest and let him examine you. Take along the offering required in the law of Moses for those who have been healed of leprosy, so everyone will have proof of your healing." ¹⁵ Yet despite Jesus' instructions, the report of his power spread even faster, and vast crowds came to hear him preach and to be healed of their diseases. ¹⁶ But Jesus often withdrew to the wilderness for prayer.

Jesus Heals a Paralysed Man

¹⁷ One day while Jesus was teaching, some Pharisees and teachers of religious law were sitting nearby. (It seemed that these men showed up from every village in all Galilee and Judea, as well as from Jerusalem.) And the Lord's healing power was strongly with Jesus. ¹⁸ Some men came carrying a paralysed man on a sleeping mat. They tried to push through the crowd to Jesus, ¹⁹ but they couldn't reach him. So they went up to the roof, took off some tiles, and lowered the sick man down into the crowd, still on his mat, right in front of Jesus. ²⁰ Seeing their faith, Jesus said to the man, "My son, your sins are forgiven."

²¹ "Who does this man think he is?" the Pharisees and teachers of religious law said to each other. "This is blasphemy! Who but God can forgive sins?"

²² Jesus knew what they were thinking, so he asked them, "Why do you think this is blasphemy? ²³ Is it easier to say, 'Your sins are forgiven' or 'Get up and walk'? ²⁴ I will prove that I, the Son of Man, have the authority on earth to forgive sins." Then Jesus turned to the paralysed man and said, "Stand up, take your mat, and go on home, because you are healed!"

²⁵ And immediately, as everyone watched, the man jumped to his feet, picked up his mat, and went home praising God. ²⁶ Everyone was gripped with great wonder and awe. And they praised God, saying over and over again, "We have seen amazing things today."

Jesus Calls Levi (Matthew)

²⁷ Later, as Jesus left the town, he saw a tax collector named Levi sitting at his tax-collection booth. "Come, be my disciple!" Jesus said to him. ²⁸ So Levi got up, left everything, and followed him.

²⁹ Soon Levi held a banquet in his home with Jesus as the guest of honour. Many of Levi's fellow tax collectors and other guests were there. ³⁰ But the Pharisees and their teachers of religious law complained bitterly to Jesus' disciples, "Why do you eat and drink with such scum*?"

³¹ Jesus answered them, "Healthy people don't need a doctor—sick people do. ³² I have come to call sinners to turn from their sins, not to spend my time with those who think they are already good enough."

A Discussion about Fasting

³³ The religious leaders complained that Jesus' disciples were feasting instead of fasting. "John the Baptist's disciples always fast and pray," they declared, "and so do the disciples of the Pharisees. Why are yours always feasting?"

³⁴ Jesus asked, "Do wedding guests fast while celebrating with the groom? ³⁵ Someday he will be taken away from them, and then they will fast."

³⁶ Then Jesus gave them this illustration: "No one tears a piece of cloth from a new garment and uses it to patch an old garment. For then the new garment would be torn, and the patch wouldn't even match the old garment. ³⁷ And no one puts new wine into old wineskins. The new wine would burst the old skins, spilling the wine and ruining the skins. ³⁸ New wine must be put into new wineskins. ³⁹ But no one who drinks the old wine seems to want the fresh and the new. 'The old is better,' they say."

CHAPTER 6

A Discussion about the Sabbath

One Sabbath day as Jesus was walking through some cornfields, his disciples broke off heads of wheat, rubbed off the husks in their hands, and ate the grain. ² But some Pharisees said, "You shouldn't be doing that! It's against the law to work by harvesting corn on the Sabbath."

³ Jesus replied, "Haven't you ever read in the Scriptures what King David did when he and his companions were hungry? ⁴ He went into the house of God, ate the special bread reserved for the priests alone, and then gave some to his friends. That was breaking the law, too." ⁵ And Jesus added, "I, the Son of Man, am master even of the Sabbath."

Jesus Heals on the Sabbath

⁶ On another Sabbath day, a man with a deformed right hand was in the synagogue while Jesus was teaching. ⁷ The teachers of religious law and the Pharisees watched

closely to see whether Jesus would heal the man on the Sabbath, because they were eager to find some legal charge to bring against him. ⁸But Jesus knew their thoughts. He said to the man with the deformed hand, "Come and stand here where everyone can see." So the man came forward. ⁹Then Jesus said to his critics, "I have a question for you. Is it legal to do good deeds on the Sabbath, or is it a day for doing harm? Is this a day to save life or to destroy it?" ¹⁰He looked around at them one by one and then said to the man, "Reach out your hand." The man reached out his hand, and it became normal again! ¹¹At this, the enemies of Jesus were wild with rage and began to discuss what to do with him.

Jesus Chooses the Twelve Apostles

¹²One day soon afterwards Jesus went to a mountain to pray, and he prayed to God all night. ¹³At daybreak he called together all of his disciples and chose twelve of them to be apostles. Here are their names:
¹⁴Simon (he also called him Peter),

Andrew (Peter's brother),
James,
John,
Philip,
Bartholomew,
¹⁵Matthew,
Thomas,
James (son of Alphaeus),
Simon (the Zealot),
¹⁶Judas (son of James),
Judas Iscariot (who later betrayed him).

Crowds Follow Jesus

¹⁷When they came down the slopes of the mountain, the disciples stood with Jesus on a large, level area, surrounded by many of his followers and by the crowds. There were people from all over Judea and from Jerusalem and from as far north as the seacoasts of Tyre and Sidon. ¹⁸They had come to hear him and to be healed, and Jesus cast out many evil spirits. ¹⁹Everyone was trying to touch him, because healing power went out from him, and they were all cured.

The Beatitudes

²⁰Then Jesus turned to his disciples and said,
  "God blesses you who are poor,
    for the Kingdom of God is given to you.
²¹God blesses you who are hungry now,
    for you will be satisfied.
  God blesses you who weep now,
    for the time will come when you will laugh with joy.
²²God blesses you who are hated and excluded and
      mocked and cursed
    because you are identified with me, the Son of Man.
²³"When that happens, rejoice! Yes, leap for joy! For a great reward awaits you in heaven. And remember, the ancient prophets were also treated that way by your ancestors.

Sorrows Foretold

²⁴"What sorrows await you who are rich,
    for you have your only happiness now.
²⁵What sorrows await you who are satisfied and
      prosperous now,
    for a time of awful hunger is before you.

What sorrows await you who laugh carelessly,
    for your laughing will turn to mourning and sorrow.
²⁶ What sorrows await you who are praised by the crowds,
    for their ancestors also praised false prophets.

Love for Enemies

²⁷ "But if you are willing to listen, I say, love your enemies. Do good to those who hate you. ²⁸ Pray for the happiness of those who curse you. Pray for those who hurt you. ²⁹ If someone slaps you on one cheek, turn the other cheek. If someone demands your coat, offer your shirt also. ³⁰ Give what you have to anyone who asks you for it; and when things are taken away from you, don't try to get them back. ³¹ Do for others as you would like them to do for you.

³² "Do you think you deserve credit merely for loving those who love you? Even the sinners do that! ³³ And if you do good only to those who do good to you, is that so wonderful? Even sinners do that much! ³⁴ And if you lend money only to those who can repay you, what good is that? Even sinners will lend to their own kind for a full return.

³⁵ "Love your enemies! Do good to them! Lend to them! And don't be concerned that they might not repay. Then your reward from heaven will be very great, and you will truly be acting as children of the Most High, for he is kind to the unthankful and to those who are wicked. ³⁶ You must be compassionate, just as your Father is compassionate.

Don't Condemn Others

37 "Stop judging others, and you will not be judged. Stop criticizing others, or it will all come back on you. If you forgive others, you will be forgiven. 38 If you give, you will receive. Your gift will return to you in full measure, pressed down, shaken together to make room for more, and running over. Whatever measure you use in giving—large or small—it will be used to measure what is given back to you."

39 Then Jesus gave the following illustration: "What good is it for one blind person to lead another? The first one will fall into a ditch and pull the other down also. 40 A student is not greater than the teacher. But the student who works hard will become like the teacher.

41 "And why worry about a speck in your friend's eye* when you have a log in your own? 42 How can you think of saying, 'Friend,* let me help you get rid of that speck in your eye,' when you can't see past the log in your own eye? Hypocrite! First get rid of the log from your own eye; then perhaps you will see well enough to deal with the speck in your friend's eye.

The Tree and Its Fruit

43 "A good tree can't produce bad fruit, and a bad tree can't produce good fruit. 44 A tree is identified by the kind of fruit it produces. Figs never grow on thorn bushes or grapes on bramble bushes. 45 A good person produces good deeds from a good heart, and an evil person produces evil deeds from an evil heart. Whatever is in your heart determines what you say.

Building on a Solid Foundation

⁴⁶ "So why do you call me 'Lord,' when you won't obey me? ⁴⁷ I will show you what it's like when someone comes to me, listens to my teaching, and then obeys me. ⁴⁸ It is like a person who builds a house on a strong foundation laid upon the underlying rock. When the floodwaters rise and break against the house, it stands firm because it is well built. ⁴⁹ But anyone who listens and doesn't obey is like a person who builds a house without a foundation. When the floods sweep down against that house, it will crumble into a heap of ruins."

CHAPTER 7

Faith of the Roman Officer

When Jesus had finished saying all this, he went back to Capernaum. ² Now the highly valued slave of a Roman officer was sick and near death. ³ When the officer heard about Jesus, he sent some respected Jewish leaders to ask him to come and heal his slave. ⁴ So they earnestly begged Jesus to come with them and help the man. "If anyone deserves your help, it is he," they said, ⁵ "for he loves the Jews and even built a synagogue for us."

⁶ So Jesus went with them. But just before they arrived at the house, the officer sent some friends to say, "Lord, don't trouble yourself by coming to my home, for I am not worthy of such an honour. ⁷ I am not even worthy to come and meet you. Just say the word from where you are, and my servant will be healed. ⁸ I know because I am

under the authority of my superior officers, and I have authority over my soldiers. I only need to say, 'Go,' and they go, or 'Come,' and they come. And if I say to my slaves, 'Do this or that,' they do it."

⁹When Jesus heard this, he was amazed. Turning to the crowd, he said, "I tell you, I haven't seen faith like this in all the land of Israel!" ¹⁰And when the officer's friends returned to his house, they found the slave completely healed.

Jesus Raises a Widow's Son

¹¹Soon afterwards Jesus went with his disciples to the village of Nain, with a great crowd following him. ¹²A funeral procession was coming out as he approached the village gate. The boy who had died was the only son of a widow, and many mourners from the village were with her. ¹³When the Lord saw her, his heart overflowed with compassion. "Don't cry!" he said. ¹⁴Then he walked over to the coffin and touched it, and the bearers stopped. "Young man," he said, "get up." ¹⁵Then the dead boy sat up and began to talk to those around him! And Jesus gave him back to his mother.

¹⁶Great fear swept the crowd, and they praised God, saying, "A mighty prophet has risen among us," and "We have seen the hand of God at work today." ¹⁷The report of what Jesus had done that day spread all over Judea and even out across its borders.

Jesus and John the Baptist

¹⁸The disciples of John the Baptist told John about everything Jesus was doing. So John called for two of

his disciples, [19]and he sent them to the Lord to ask him, "Are you the Messiah we've been expecting, or should we keep looking for someone else?"

[20]John's two disciples found Jesus and said to him, "John the Baptist sent us to ask, 'Are you the Messiah we've been expecting, or should we keep looking for someone else?'"

[21]At that very time, he cured many people of their various diseases, and he cast out evil spirits and restored sight to the blind. [22]Then he told John's disciples, "Go back to John and tell him what you have seen and heard—the blind see, the lame walk, the lepers are cured, the deaf hear, the dead are raised to life, and the Good News is being preached to the poor. [23]And tell him, 'God blesses those who are not offended by me.*'"

[24]After they left, Jesus talked to the crowd about John. "Who is this man in the wilderness that you went out to see? Did you find him weak as a reed, moved by every breath of wind? [25]Or were you expecting to see a man dressed in expensive clothes? No, people who wear beautiful clothes and live in luxury are found in palaces, not in the wilderness. [26]Were you looking for a prophet? Yes, and he is more than a prophet. [27]John is the man to whom the Scriptures refer when they say,

'Look, I am sending my messenger before you,
    and he will prepare your way before you.'*

[28]I tell you, of all who have ever lived, none is greater than John. Yet even the most insignificant person in the Kingdom of God is greater than he is!"

[29]When they heard this, all the people, including the unjust tax collectors, agreed that God's plan was right,* for they had been baptized by John. [30]But the Pharisees

and experts in religious law had rejected God's plan for them, for they had refused John's baptism.

³¹ "How shall I describe this generation?" Jesus asked. "With what will I compare them? ³² They are like a group of children playing a game in the public square. They complain to their friends, 'We played wedding songs, and you weren't happy, so we played funeral songs, but you weren't sad.' ³³ For John the Baptist didn't drink wine and he often fasted, and you say, 'He's demon-possessed.' ³⁴ And I, the Son of Man, feast and drink, and you say, 'He's a glutton and a drunkard, and a friend of the worst sort of sinners!' ³⁵ But wisdom is shown to be right by the lives of those who follow it.*"

Jesus Anointed by a Sinful Woman

³⁶ One of the Pharisees asked Jesus to come to his home for a meal, so Jesus accepted the invitation and sat down to eat. ³⁷ A certain immoral woman heard he was there and brought a beautiful jar* filled with expensive perfume. ³⁸ Then she knelt behind him at his feet, weeping. Her tears fell on his feet, and she wiped them off with her hair. Then she kept kissing his feet and putting perfume on them.

³⁹ When the Pharisee who was the host saw what was happening and who the woman was, he said to himself, "This proves that Jesus is no prophet. If God had really sent him, he would know what kind of woman is touching him. She's a sinner!"

⁴⁰ Then Jesus spoke up and answered his thoughts. "Simon," he said to the Pharisee, "I have something to say to you."

"All right, Teacher," Simon replied, "go ahead."

⁴¹ Then Jesus told him this story: "A man loaned money to two people—five hundred pieces of silver* to one and fifty pieces to the other. ⁴² But neither of them could repay him, so he kindly forgave them both, cancelling their debts. Who do you suppose loved him more after that?"

⁴³ Simon answered, "I suppose the one for whom he cancelled the larger debt."

"That's right," Jesus said. ⁴⁴ Then he turned to the woman and said to Simon, "Look at this woman kneeling here. When I entered your home, you didn't offer me water to wash the dust from my feet, but she has washed them with her tears and wiped them with her hair. ⁴⁵ You didn't give me a kiss of greeting, but she has kissed my feet again and again from the time I first came in. ⁴⁶ You neglected the courtesy of olive oil to anoint my head, but she has anointed my feet with rare perfume. ⁴⁷ I tell you, her sins —and they are many— have been forgiven, so she has shown me much love. But a person who is forgiven little shows only little love." ⁴⁸ Then Jesus said to the woman, "Your sins are forgiven."

⁴⁹ The men at the table said among themselves, "Who does this man think he is, going around forgiving sins?"

⁵⁰ And Jesus said to the woman, "Your faith has saved you; go in peace."

CHAPTER 8

Women Who Followed Jesus

Not long afterwards Jesus began a tour of the nearby cities and villages to announce the Good News concerning the Kingdom of God. He took his twelve disciples with him, ² along with some women he had healed and from whom he had cast out evil spirits. Among them were Mary Magdalene, from whom he had cast out seven demons; ³ Joanna, the wife of Chuza, Herod's business manager; Susanna; and many others who were contributing from their own resources to support Jesus and his disciples.

Story of the Farmer Scattering Seed

⁴ One day Jesus told this story to a large crowd that had gathered from many towns to hear him: ⁵ "A farmer went out to plant some seed. As he scattered it across his field, some seed fell on a footpath, where it was stepped on, and the birds came and ate it. ⁶ Other seed fell on shallow soil with underlying rock. This seed began to grow, but soon it withered and died for lack of moisture. ⁷ Other seed fell among thorns that shot up and choked out the tender blades. ⁸ Still other seed fell on fertile soil. This seed grew and produced a crop one hundred times as much as had been planted." When he had said this, he called out, "Anyone who is willing to hear should listen and understand!"

⁹ His disciples asked him what the story meant. ¹⁰ He replied, "You have been permitted to understand the secrets of the Kingdom of God. But I am using these stories to conceal everything about it from outsiders, so that the Scriptures might be fulfilled:

'They see what I do,
    but they don't really see;
they hear what I say,
    but they don't understand.'*

¹¹ "This is the meaning of the story: The seed is God's message. ¹² The seed that fell on the hard path represents those who hear the message, but then the Devil comes and steals it away and prevents them from believing and being saved. ¹³ The rocky soil represents those who hear the message with joy. But like young plants in such soil, their roots don't go very deep. They believe for a while, but they wilt when the hot winds of testing blow. ¹⁴ The thorny ground represents those who hear and accept the message, but all too quickly the message is crowded out by the cares and riches and pleasures of this life. And so they never grow into maturity. ¹⁵ But the good soil represents honest, good-hearted people who hear God's message, cling to it, and steadily produce a huge harvest.

Illustration of the Lamp

¹⁶ "No one would light a lamp and then cover it up or put it under a bed. No, lamps are mounted in the open, where they can be seen by those entering the house. ¹⁷ For everything that is hidden or secret will eventually be brought to light and made plain to all. ¹⁸ So be sure to pay attention to what you hear. To those who are open to my teaching, more understanding will be given. But to those who are not listening, even what they think they have will be taken away from them."

The True Family of Jesus

¹⁹ Once when Jesus' mother and brothers came to see him, they couldn't get to him because of the crowds.

²⁰ Someone told Jesus, "Your mother and your brothers are outside, and they want to see you."

²¹ Jesus replied, "My mother and my brothers are all those who hear the message of God and obey it."

Jesus Calms the Storm

²² One day Jesus said to his disciples, "Let's cross over to the other side of the lake." So they got into a boat and started out. ²³ On the way across, Jesus lay down for a nap, and while he was sleeping the wind began to rise. A fierce storm developed that threatened to swamp them, and they were in real danger.

²⁴ The disciples woke him up, shouting, "Master, Master, we're going to drown!"

So Jesus rebuked the wind and the raging waves. The storm stopped and all was calm! ²⁵ Then he asked them, "Where is your faith?"

And they were filled with awe and amazement. They said to one another, "Who is this man, that even the winds and waves obey him?"

Jesus Heals a Demon-Possessed Man

²⁶ So they arrived in the land of the Gerasenes,* across the lake from Galilee. ²⁷ As Jesus was climbing out of the boat, a man who was possessed by demons came out to meet him. Homeless and naked, he had lived in a cemetery for a long time. ²⁸ As soon as he saw Jesus, he shrieked and fell to the ground before him, screaming, "Why are you bothering me, Jesus, Son of the Most High God? Please, I beg you, don't torture me!" ²⁹ For Jesus had already commanded the evil spirit to come out of him. This spirit

had often taken control of the man. Even when he was shackled with chains, he simply broke them and rushed out into the wilderness, completely under the demon's power.

³⁰ "What is your name?" Jesus asked.

"Legion," he replied—for the man was filled with many demons. ³¹ The demons kept begging Jesus not to send them into the Bottomless Pit. ³² A large herd of pigs was feeding on the hillside nearby, and the demons pleaded with him to let them enter into the pigs. Jesus gave them permission. ³³ So the demons came out of the man and entered the pigs, and the whole herd plunged down the steep hillside into the lake, where they drowned.

³⁴ When the herdsmen saw it, they fled to the nearby city and the surrounding countryside, spreading the news as they ran. ³⁵ A crowd soon gathered around Jesus, for they wanted to see for themselves what had happened. And they saw the man who had been possessed by demons sitting quietly at Jesus' feet, clothed and sane. And the whole crowd was afraid. ³⁶ Then those who had seen what happened told the others how the demon-possessed man had been healed. ³⁷ And all the people in that region begged Jesus to go away and leave them alone, for a great wave of fear swept over them.

So Jesus returned to the boat and left, crossing back to the other side of the lake. ³⁸ The man who had been demon-possessed begged to go, too, but Jesus said, ³⁹ "No, go back to your family and tell them all the wonderful things God has done for you." So he went all through the city telling about the great thing Jesus had done for him.

Jesus Heals in Response to Faith

⁴⁰ On the other side of the lake the crowds received Jesus with open arms because they had been waiting for him. ⁴¹ And now a man named Jairus, a leader of the local synagogue, came and fell down at Jesus' feet, begging him to come home with him. ⁴² His only child was dying, a little girl twelve years old.

As Jesus went with him, he was surrounded by the crowds. ⁴³ And there was a woman in the crowd who had had a haemorrhage for twelve years. She had spent everything she had on doctors* and still could find no cure. ⁴⁴ She came up behind Jesus and touched the fringe of his robe. Immediately, the bleeding stopped.

⁴⁵ "Who touched me?" Jesus asked.

Everyone denied it, and Peter said, "Master, this whole crowd is pressing up against you."

⁴⁶ But Jesus told him, "No, someone deliberately touched me, for I felt healing power go out from me." ⁴⁷ When the woman realized that Jesus knew, she began to tremble and fell to her knees before him. The whole crowd heard her explain why she had touched him and that she had been immediately healed. ⁴⁸ "Daughter," he said to her, "your faith has made you well. Go in peace."

⁴⁹ While he was still speaking to her, a messenger arrived from Jairus's home with the message, "Your little girl is dead. There's no use troubling the Teacher now."

⁵⁰ But when Jesus heard what had happened, he said to Jairus, "Don't be afraid. Just trust me, and she will be all right."

⁵¹ When they arrived at the house, Jesus wouldn't let anyone go in with him except Peter, James, John, and the little girl's father and mother. ⁵² The house was filled

with people weeping and wailing, but he said, "Stop the weeping! She isn't dead; she is only asleep."

⁵³ But the crowd laughed at him because they all knew she had died. ⁵⁴ Then Jesus took her by the hand and said in a loud voice, "Get up, my child!" ⁵⁵ And at that moment her life returned, and she immediately stood up! Then Jesus told them to give her something to eat. ⁵⁶ Her parents were overwhelmed, but Jesus insisted that they tell nobody what had happened.

CHAPTER 9

Jesus Sends Out the Twelve Apostles

One day Jesus called together his twelve apostles and gave them power and authority to cast out demons and to heal all diseases. ² Then he sent them out to tell everyone about the coming of the Kingdom of God and to heal the sick. ³ "Don't even take along a walking stick," he instructed them, "nor a traveller's bag, nor food, nor money. Not even an extra coat. ⁴ When you enter each village, be a guest in only one home. ⁵ If the people of the village won't receive your message when you enter it, shake off its dust from your feet as you leave. It is a sign that you have abandoned that village to its fate."

⁶ So they began their circuit of the villages, preaching the Good News and healing the sick.

Herod's Confusion

⁷ When reports of Jesus' miracles reached Herod Antipas,* he was worried and puzzled because some

were saying, "This is John the Baptist come back to life again." ⁸Others were saying, "It is Elijah or some other ancient prophet risen from the dead."

⁹"I beheaded John," Herod said, "so who is this man about whom I hear such strange stories?" And he tried to see him.

Jesus Feeds Five Thousand

¹⁰When the apostles returned, they told Jesus everything they had done. Then he slipped quietly away with them towards the town of Bethsaida. ¹¹But the crowds found out where he was going, and they followed him. And he welcomed them, teaching them about the Kingdom of God and curing those who were ill. ¹²Late in the afternoon the twelve disciples came to him and said, "Send the crowds away to the nearby villages and farms, so they can find food and lodging for the night. There is nothing to eat here in this deserted place."

¹³But Jesus said, "You feed them."

"Impossible!" they protested. "We have only five loaves of bread and two fish. Or are you expecting us to go and buy enough food for this whole crowd?" ¹⁴For there were about five thousand men there.

"Just tell them to sit down on the ground in groups of about fifty each," Jesus replied. ¹⁵So the people all sat down. ¹⁶Jesus took the five loaves and two fish, looked up towards heaven, and asked God's blessing on the food. Breaking the loaves into pieces, he kept giving the bread and fish to the disciples to give to the people. ¹⁷They all ate as much as they wanted, and they picked up twelve baskets of leftovers!

Peter's Declaration about Jesus

¹⁸ One day as Jesus was alone, praying, he came over to his disciples and asked them, "Who do people say I am?"

¹⁹ "Well," they replied, "some say John the Baptist, some say Elijah, and others say you are one of the other ancient prophets risen from the dead."

²⁰ Then he asked them, "Who do you say I am?"

Peter replied, "You are the Messiah sent from God!"

Jesus Predicts His Death

²¹ Jesus warned them not to tell anyone about this. ²² "For I, the Son of Man, must suffer many terrible things," he said. "I will be rejected by the leaders, the leading priests, and the teachers of religious law. I will be killed, but three days later I will be raised from the dead."

²³ Then he said to the crowd, "If any of you wants to be my follower, you must put aside your selfish ambition, shoulder your cross daily, and follow me. ²⁴ If you try to keep your life for yourself, you will lose it. But if you give up your life for me, you will find true life. ²⁵ And how do you benefit if you gain the whole world but lose or forfeit your own soul in the process? ²⁶ If a person is ashamed of me and my message, I, the Son of Man, will be ashamed of that person when I return in my glory and in the glory of the Father and the holy angels. ²⁷ And I assure you that some of you standing here right now will not die before you see the Kingdom of God."

The Transfiguration

²⁸ About eight days later Jesus took Peter, James, and John to a mountain to pray. ²⁹ And as he was praying,

the appearance of his face changed, and his clothing became dazzling white. ³⁰ Then two men, Moses and Elijah, appeared and began talking with Jesus. ³¹ They were glorious to see. And they were speaking of how he was about to fulfil God's plan by dying in Jerusalem.

³² Peter and the others were very drowsy and had fallen asleep. Now they woke up and saw Jesus' glory and the two men standing with him. ³³ As Moses and Elijah were starting to leave, Peter, not even knowing what he was saying, blurted out, "Master, this is wonderful! We will make three shrines*—one for you, one for Moses, and one for Elijah." ³⁴ But even as he was saying this, a cloud came over them; and terror gripped them as it covered them.

³⁵ Then a voice from the cloud said, "This is my Son, my Chosen One.* Listen to him." ³⁶ When the voice died away, Jesus was there alone. They didn't tell anyone what they had seen until long after this happened.

Jesus Heals a Demon-Possessed Boy

³⁷ The next day, after they had come down the mountain, a huge crowd met Jesus. ³⁸ A man in the crowd called out to him, "Teacher, look at my boy, who is my only son. ³⁹ An evil spirit keeps seizing him, making him scream. It throws him into convulsions so that he foams at the mouth. It is always hitting and injuring him. It hardly ever leaves him alone. ⁴⁰ I begged your disciples to cast the spirit out, but they couldn't do it."

⁴¹ "You stubborn, faithless people," Jesus said, "how long must I be with you and put up with you? Bring him here." ⁴² As the boy came forward, the demon

knocked him to the ground and threw him into a violent convulsion. But Jesus rebuked the evil spirit and healed the boy. Then he gave him back to his father. ⁴³ Awe gripped the people as they saw this display of God's power.

Jesus Again Predicts His Death

While everyone was marvelling over all the wonderful things he was doing, Jesus said to his disciples, ⁴⁴ "Listen to me and remember what I say. The Son of Man is going to be betrayed." ⁴⁵ But they didn't know what he meant. Its significance was hidden from them, so they could not understand it, and they were afraid to ask him about it.

The Greatest in the Kingdom

⁴⁶ Then there was an argument among them as to which of them would be the greatest. ⁴⁷ But Jesus knew their thoughts, so he brought a little child to his side. ⁴⁸ Then he said to them, "Anyone who welcomes a little child like this on my behalf welcomes me, and anyone who welcomes me welcomes my Father who sent me. Whoever is the least among you is the greatest."

Using the Name of Jesus

⁴⁹ John said to Jesus, "Master, we saw someone using your name to cast out demons. We tried to stop him because he isn't in our group."

⁵⁰ But Jesus said, "Don't stop him! Anyone who is not against you is for you."

Opposition from Samaritans

⁵¹ As the time drew near for his return to heaven, Jesus resolutely set out for Jerusalem. ⁵² He sent messengers ahead to a Samaritan village to prepare for his arrival. ⁵³ But they were turned away. The people of the village refused to have anything to do with Jesus because he had resolved to go to Jerusalem. ⁵⁴ When James and John heard about it, they said to Jesus, "Lord, should we order down fire from heaven to burn them up*?" ⁵⁵ But Jesus turned and rebuked them.* ⁵⁶ So they went on to another village.

The Cost of Following Jesus

⁵⁷ As they were walking along someone said to Jesus, "I will follow you no matter where you go."

⁵⁸ But Jesus replied, "Foxes have dens to live in, and birds have nests, but I, the Son of Man, have no home of my own, not even a place to lay my head."

⁵⁹ He said to another person, "Come, be my disciple."

The man agreed, but he said, "Lord, first let me return home and bury my father."

⁶⁰ Jesus replied, "Let those who are spiritually dead look after their own dead.* Your duty is to go and preach the coming of the Kingdom of God."

⁶¹ Another said, "Yes, Lord, I will follow you, but first let me say goodbye to my family."

⁶² But Jesus told him, "Anyone who puts a hand to the plough and then looks back is not fit for the Kingdom of God."

CHAPTER 10

Jesus Sends Out His Disciples

The Lord now chose seventy-two* other disciples and sent them on ahead in pairs to all the towns and villages he planned to visit. ²These were his instructions to them: "The harvest is so great, but the workers are so few. Pray to the Lord who is in charge of the harvest, and ask him to send out more workers for his fields. ³Go now, and remember that I am sending you out as lambs among wolves. ⁴Don't take along any money, or a traveller's bag, or even an extra pair of sandals. And don't stop to greet anyone on the road.

⁵"Whenever you enter a home, give it your blessing. ⁶If those who live there are worthy, the blessing will stand; if they are not, the blessing will return to you. ⁷When you enter a town, don't move around from home to home. Stay in one place, eating and drinking what they provide for you. Don't hesitate to accept hospitality, because those who work deserve their pay.

⁸"If a town welcomes you, eat whatever is set before you ⁹and heal the sick. As you heal them, say, 'The Kingdom of God is near you now.' ¹⁰But if a town refuses to welcome you, go out into its streets and say, ¹¹'We wipe the dust of your town from our feet as a public announcement of your doom. And don't forget the Kingdom of God is near!' ¹²The truth is, even wicked Sodom will be better off than such a town on the judgement day.

¹³"What horrors await you, Korazin and Bethsaida! For if the miracles I did in you had been done in wicked Tyre

and Sidon, their people would have sat in deep repentance long ago, clothed in sackcloth and throwing ashes on their heads to show their remorse. ¹⁴ Yes, Tyre and Sidon will be better off on the judgement day than you. ¹⁵ And you people of Capernaum, will you be exalted to heaven? No, you will be brought down to the place of the dead.*"

¹⁶ Then he said to the disciples, "Anyone who accepts your message is also accepting me. And anyone who rejects you is rejecting me. And anyone who rejects me is rejecting God who sent me."

¹⁷ When the seventy-two disciples returned, they joyfully reported to him, "Lord, even the demons obey us when we use your name!"

¹⁸ "Yes," he told them, "I saw Satan falling from heaven as a flash of lightning! ¹⁹ And I have given you authority over all the power of the enemy, and you can walk among snakes and scorpions and crush them. Nothing will injure you. ²⁰ But don't rejoice just because evil spirits obey you; rejoice because your names are registered as citizens of heaven."

Jesus' Prayer of Thanksgiving

²¹ Then Jesus was filled with the joy of the Holy Spirit and said, "O Father, Lord of heaven and earth, thank you for hiding the truth from those who think themselves so wise and clever, and for revealing it to the childlike. Yes, Father, it pleased you to do it this way.

²² "My Father has given me authority over everything. No one really knows the Son except the Father, and no one really knows the Father except the Son and those to whom the Son chooses to reveal him."

[23] Then when they were alone, he turned to the disciples and said, "How privileged you are to see what you have seen. [24] I tell you, many prophets and kings have longed to see and hear what you have seen and heard, but they could not."

The Most Important Commandment

[25] One day an expert in religious law stood up to test Jesus by asking him this question: "Teacher, what must I do to receive eternal life?"

[26] Jesus replied, "What does the law of Moses say? How do you read it?"

[27] The man answered, " 'You must love the Lord your God with all your heart, all your soul, all your strength, and all your mind.' And, 'Love your neighbour as yourself.' "*

[28] "Right!" Jesus told him. "Do this and you will live!"

[29] The man wanted to justify his actions, so he asked Jesus, "And who is my neighbour?"

Story of the Good Samaritan

[30] Jesus replied with an illustration: "A Jewish man was travelling on a trip from Jerusalem to Jericho, and he was attacked by bandits. They stripped him of his clothes and money, beat him up, and left him half dead beside the road.

[31] "By chance a Jewish priest came along; but when he saw the man lying there, he crossed to the other side of the road and passed him by. [32] A Temple assistant* walked over and looked at him lying there, but he also passed by on the other side.

³³ "Then a despised Samaritan came along, and when he saw the man, he felt deep pity. ³⁴ Kneeling beside him, the Samaritan soothed his wounds with medicine and bandaged them. Then he put the man on his own donkey and took him to an inn, where he took care of him. ³⁵ The next day he handed the innkeeper two pieces of silver* and told him to take care of the man. 'If his bill runs higher than that,' he said, 'I'll pay the difference the next time I am here.'

³⁶ "Now which of these three would you say was a neighbour to the man who was attacked by bandits?" Jesus asked.

³⁷ The man replied, "The one who showed him mercy." Then Jesus said, "Yes, now go and do the same."

Jesus Visits Martha and Mary

³⁸ As Jesus and the disciples continued on their way to Jerusalem, they came to a village where a woman named Martha welcomed them into her home. ³⁹ Her sister, Mary, sat at the Lord's feet, listening to what he taught. ⁴⁰ But Martha was worrying over the big dinner she was preparing. She came to Jesus and said, "Lord, doesn't it seem unfair to you that my sister just sits here while I do all the work? Tell her to come and help me."

⁴¹ But the Lord said to her, "My dear Martha, you are so upset over all these details! ⁴² There is really only one thing worth being concerned about. Mary has discovered it—and I won't take it away from her."

CHAPTER 11

Teaching about Prayer

Once when Jesus had been out praying, one of his disciples came to him as he finished and said, "Lord, teach us to pray, just as John taught his disciples."

²He said, "This is how you should pray:

"Father, may your name be honoured.
    May your Kingdom come soon.
³ Give us our food day by day.
⁴ And forgive us our sins—
    just as we forgive those who have sinned against us.
    And don't let us yield to temptation.*"

⁵Then, teaching them more about prayer, he used this illustration: "Suppose you went to a friend's house at midnight, wanting to borrow three loaves of bread. You would say to him, ⁶'A friend of mine has just arrived for a visit, and I have nothing for him to eat.' ⁷He would call out from his bedroom, 'Don't bother me. The door is locked for the night, and we are all in bed. I can't help you this time.' ⁸But I tell you this—though he won't do it as a friend, if you keep knocking long enough, he will get up and give you what you want so his reputation won't be damaged.*

⁹"And so I tell you, keep on asking, and you will be given what you ask for. Keep on looking, and you will find. Keep on knocking, and the door will be opened. ¹⁰For everyone who asks, receives. Everyone who seeks, finds. And the door is opened to everyone who knocks.

¹¹"You fathers—if your children ask* for a fish, do you give them a snake instead? ¹²Or if they ask for an egg, do

you give them a scorpion? Of course not! ¹³If you sinful people know how to give good gifts to your children, how much more will your heavenly Father give the Holy Spirit to those who ask him."

Jesus and the Prince of Demons

¹⁴One day Jesus cast a demon out of a man who couldn't speak, and the man's voice returned to him. The crowd was amazed, ¹⁵but some said, "No wonder he can cast out demons. He gets his power from Satan,* the prince of demons!" ¹⁶Trying to test Jesus, others asked for a miraculous sign from heaven to see if he was from God.

¹⁷He knew their thoughts, so he said, "Any kingdom at war with itself is doomed. A divided home is also doomed. ¹⁸You say I am empowered by the prince of demons.* But if Satan is fighting against himself by empowering me to cast out his demons, how can his kingdom survive? ¹⁹And if I am empowered by the prince of demons, what about your own followers? They cast out demons, too, so they will judge you for what you have said. ²⁰But if I am casting out demons by the power of God, then the Kingdom of God has arrived among you. ²¹For when Satan,* who is completely armed, guards his palace, it is safe—²²until someone who is stronger attacks and overpowers him, strips him of his weapons, and carries off his belongings.

²³"Anyone who isn't helping me opposes me, and anyone who isn't working with me is actually working against me.

²⁴"When an evil spirit leaves a person, it goes into the desert, searching for rest. But when it finds none, it says, 'I will return to the person I came from.' ²⁵So it returns

and finds that its former home is all swept and clean. ²⁶ Then the spirit finds seven other spirits more evil than itself, and they all enter the person and live there. And so that person is worse off than before."

²⁷ As he was speaking, a woman in the crowd called out, "God bless your mother—the womb from which you came, and the breasts that nursed you!"

²⁸ He replied, "But even more blessed are all who hear the word of God and put it into practice."

The Sign of Jonah

²⁹ As the crowd pressed in on Jesus, he said, "These are evil times, and this evil generation keeps asking me to show them a miraculous sign. But the only sign I will give them is the sign of the prophet Jonah. ³⁰ What happened to him was a sign to the people of Nineveh that God had sent him. What happens to me will be a sign that God has sent me, the Son of Man, to these people.

³¹ "The queen of Sheba* will rise up against this generation on judgement day and condemn it, because she came from a distant land to hear the wisdom of Solomon. And now someone greater than Solomon is here—and you refuse to listen to him. ³² The people of Nineveh, too, will rise up against this generation on judgement day and condemn it, because they repented at the preaching of Jonah. And now someone greater than Jonah is here—and you refuse to repent.

Receiving the Light

³³ "No one lights a lamp and then hides it or puts it under a basket. Instead, it is put on a lampstand to give light to

all who enter the room. ³⁴ Your eye is a lamp for your body. A pure eye lets sunshine into your soul. But an evil eye shuts out the light and plunges you into darkness. ³⁵ Make sure that the light you think you have is not really darkness. ³⁶ If you are filled with light, with no dark corners, then your whole life will be radiant, as though a floodlight is shining on you."

Jesus Criticizes the Religious Leaders

³⁷ As Jesus was speaking, one of the Pharisees invited him home for a meal. So he went in and took his place at the table. ³⁸ His host was amazed to see that he sat down to eat without first performing the ceremonial washing required by Jewish custom. ³⁹ Then the Lord said to him, "You Pharisees are so careful to clean the outside of the cup and the dish, but inside you are still filthy—full of greed and wickedness! ⁴⁰ Fools! Didn't God make the inside as well as the outside? ⁴¹ So give to the needy what you greedily possess, and you will be clean all over.

⁴² "But how terrible it will be for you Pharisees! For you are careful to tithe even the tiniest part of your income,* but you completely forget about justice and the love of God. You should tithe, yes, but you should not leave undone the more important things.

⁴³ "How terrible it will be for you Pharisees! For how you love the seats of honour in the synagogues and the respectful greetings from everyone as you walk through the markets! ⁴⁴ Yes, how terrible it will be for you. For you are like hidden graves in a field. People walk over them without knowing the corruption they are stepping on."

⁴⁵ "Teacher," said an expert in religious law, "you have insulted us, too, in what you just said."

⁴⁶ "Yes," said Jesus, "how terrible it will be for you experts in religious law! For you crush people beneath impossible religious demands, and you never lift a finger to help ease the burden. ⁴⁷ How terrible it will be for you! For you build tombs for the very prophets your ancestors killed long ago. ⁴⁸ Murderers! You agree with your ancestors that what they did was right. You would have done the same yourselves. ⁴⁹ This is what God in his wisdom said about you:* 'I will send prophets and apostles to them, and they will kill some and persecute the others.'

⁵⁰ "And you of this generation will be held responsible for the murder of all God's prophets from the creation of the world—⁵¹ from the murder of Abel to the murder of Zechariah, who was killed between the altar and the sanctuary. Yes, it will surely be charged against you.

⁵² "How terrible it will be for you experts in religious law! For you hide the key to knowledge from the people. You don't enter the Kingdom yourselves, and you prevent others from entering."

⁵³ As Jesus finished speaking, the Pharisees and teachers of religious law were furious. From that time on they grilled him with many hostile questions, ⁵⁴ trying to trap him into saying something they could use against him.

CHAPTER 12

A Warning against Hypocrisy

Meanwhile, the crowds grew until thousands were milling about and crushing each other. Jesus turned first to his disciples and warned them, "Beware of the yeast of the Pharisees—beware of their hypocrisy. ²The time is coming when everything will be revealed; all that is secret will be made public. ³Whatever you have said in the dark will be heard in the light, and what you have whispered behind closed doors will be shouted from the housetops for all to hear!

⁴"Dear friends, don't be afraid of those who want to kill you. They can only kill the body; they cannot do any more to you. ⁵But I'll tell you whom to fear. Fear God, who has the power to kill people and then throw them into hell.

⁶"What is the price of five sparrows? A couple of pennies? Yet God does not forget a single one of them. ⁷And the very hairs on your head are all numbered. So don't be afraid; you are more valuable to him than a whole flock of sparrows.

⁸"And I assure you of this: If anyone acknowledges me publicly here on earth, I, the Son of Man, will openly acknowledge that person in the presence of God's angels. ⁹But if anyone denies me here on earth, I will deny that person before God's angels. ¹⁰Yet those who speak against the Son of Man may be forgiven, but anyone who speaks blasphemies against the Holy Spirit will never be forgiven.

¹¹"And when you are brought to trial in the synagogues and before rulers and authorities, don't worry about what

to say in your defence, [12] for the Holy Spirit will teach you what needs to be said even as you are standing there."

Story of the Rich Fool

[13] Then someone called from the crowd, "Teacher, please tell my brother to divide our father's estate with me."

[14] Jesus replied, "Friend, who made me a judge over you to decide such things as that?" [15] Then he said, "Beware! Don't be greedy for what you don't have. Real life is not measured by how much we own."

[16] And he gave an illustration: "A rich man had a fertile farm that produced fine crops. [17] In fact, his barns were full to overflowing. [18] So he said, 'I know! I'll tear down my barns and build bigger ones. Then I'll have room enough to store everything. [19] And I'll sit back and say to myself: My friend, you have enough stored away for years to come. Now take it easy! Eat, drink, and be merry!'

[20] "But God said to him, 'You fool! You will die this very night. Then who will get it all?'

[21] "Yes, a person is a fool to store up earthly wealth but not have a rich relationship with God."

Teaching about Money and Possessions

[22] Then turning to his disciples, Jesus said, "So I tell you, don't worry about everyday life—whether you have enough food to eat or clothes to wear. [23] For life consists of far more than food and clothing. [24] Look at the ravens. They don't need to plant or harvest or put food in barns because God feeds them. And you are far more valuable to him than any birds! [25] Can all your worries add a single moment to your

life? Of course not! ²⁶ And if worry can't do little things like that, what's the use of worrying over bigger things?

²⁷ "Look at the lilies and how they grow. They don't work or make their clothing, yet Solomon in all his glory was not dressed as beautifully as they are. ²⁸ And if God cares so wonderfully for flowers that are here today and gone tomorrow, won't he more surely care for you? You have so little faith! ²⁹ And don't worry about food—what to eat and drink. Don't worry whether God will provide it for you. ³⁰ These things dominate the thoughts of most people, but your Father already knows your needs. ³¹ He will give you all you need from day to day if you make the Kingdom of God your primary concern.

³² "So don't be afraid, little flock. For it gives your Father great happiness to give you the Kingdom.

³³ "Sell what you have and give to those in need. This will store up treasure for you in heaven! And the purses of heaven have no holes in them. Your treasure will be safe—no thief can steal it and no moth can destroy it. ³⁴ Wherever your treasure is, there your heart and thoughts will also be.

Be Ready for the Lord's Coming

³⁵ "Be dressed for service and well prepared, ³⁶ as though you were waiting for your master to return from the wedding feast. Then you will be ready to open the door and let him in the moment he arrives and knocks. ³⁷ There will be special favour for those who are ready and waiting for his return. I tell you, he himself will seat them, put on an apron, and serve them as they sit and eat! ³⁸ He may come in the middle of the night or just before

dawn.* But whenever he comes, there will be special favour for his servants who are ready!

39 "Know this: A home-owner who knew exactly when a burglar was coming would not permit the house to be broken into. 40 You must be ready all the time, for the Son of Man will come when least expected."

41 Peter asked, "Lord, is this illustration just for us or for everyone?"

42 And the Lord replied, "I'm talking to any faithful, sensible servant to whom the master gives the responsibility of managing his household and feeding his family. 43 If the master returns and finds that the servant has done a good job, there will be a reward. 44 I assure you, the master will put that servant in charge of all he owns. 45 But if the servant thinks, 'My master won't be back for a while,' and begins oppressing the other servants, partying, and getting drunk—46 well, the master will return unannounced and unexpected. He will tear the servant apart and banish him with the unfaithful. 47 The servant will be severely punished, for though he knew his duty, he refused to do it.

48 "But people who are not aware that they are doing wrong will be punished only lightly. Much is required from those to whom much is given, and much more is required from those to whom much more is given.

Jesus Causes Division

49 "I have come to bring fire to the earth, and I wish that my task were already completed! 50 There is a terrible baptism ahead of me, and I am under a heavy burden until it is accomplished. 51 Do you think I have come to bring peace to the earth? No, I have come to bring strife and division! 52 From now on families will be split apart,

three in favour of me, and two against—or the other way around. ⁵³ There will be a division between father and son, mother and daughter, mother-in-law and daughter-in-law."

⁵⁴ Then Jesus turned to the crowd and said, "When you see clouds beginning to form in the west, you say, 'Here comes a shower.' And you are right. ⁵⁵ When the south wind blows, you say, 'Today will be a scorcher.' And it is. ⁵⁶ You hypocrites! You know how to interpret the appearance of the earth and the sky, but you can't interpret these present times.

⁵⁷ "Why can't you decide for yourselves what is right? ⁵⁸ If you are on the way to court and you meet your accuser, try to settle the matter before it reaches the judge, or you may be sentenced and handed over to an officer and thrown into jail. ⁵⁹ And if that happens, you won't be free again until you have paid the last penny."

CHAPTER 13

A Call to Repentance

About this time Jesus was informed that Pilate had murdered some people from Galilee as they were sacrificing at the Temple in Jerusalem. ² "Do you think those Galileans were worse sinners than other people from Galilee?" he asked. "Is that why they suffered? ³ Not at all! And you will also perish unless you turn from your evil ways and turn to God. ⁴ And what about the eighteen men who died when the Tower of Siloam fell on them? Were they the worst sinners in Jerusalem? ⁵ No, and I tell you again that unless you repent, you will also perish."

Illustration of the Barren Fig Tree

⁶ Then Jesus used this illustration: "A man planted a fig tree in his garden and came again and again to see if there was any fruit on it, but he was always disappointed. ⁷ Finally, he said to his gardener, 'I've waited three years, and there hasn't been a single fig! Cut it down. It's taking up space we can use for something else.'

⁸ "The gardener answered, 'Give it one more chance. Leave it another year, and I'll give it special attention and plenty of fertilizer. ⁹ If we get figs next year, fine. If not, you can cut it down.'"

Jesus Heals on the Sabbath

¹⁰ One Sabbath day as Jesus was teaching in a synagogue, ¹¹ he saw a woman who had been crippled by an evil spirit. She had been bent double for eighteen years and was unable to stand up straight. ¹² When Jesus saw her, he called her over and said, "Woman, you are healed of your sickness!" ¹³ Then he touched her, and instantly she could stand straight. How she praised and thanked God!

¹⁴ But the leader in charge of the synagogue was indignant that Jesus had healed her on the Sabbath day. "There are six days of the week for working," he said to the crowd. "Come on those days to be healed, not on the Sabbath."

¹⁵ But the Lord replied, "You hypocrite! You work on the Sabbath day! Don't you untie your ox or your donkey from their stalls on the Sabbath and lead them out for water? ¹⁶ Wasn't it necessary for me, even on the Sabbath day, to free this dear woman* from the bondage in which

Satan has held her for eighteen years?" ¹⁷ This shamed his enemies. And all the people rejoiced at the wonderful things he did.

Illustration of the Mustard Seed

¹⁸ Then Jesus said, "What is the Kingdom of God like? How can I illustrate it? ¹⁹ It is like a tiny mustard seed planted in a garden; it grows and becomes a tree, and the birds come and find shelter among its branches."

Illustration of the Yeast

²⁰ He also asked, "What else is the Kingdom of God like? ²¹ It is like yeast used by a woman making bread. Even though she used a large amount* of flour, the yeast permeated every part of the dough."

The Narrow Door

²² Jesus went through the towns and villages, teaching as he went, always pressing on towards Jerusalem.
²³ Someone asked him, "Lord, will only a few be saved?"

He replied, ²⁴ "The door to heaven is narrow. Work hard to get in, because many will try to enter, ²⁵ but when the head of the house has locked the door, it will be too late. Then you will stand outside knocking and pleading, 'Lord, open the door for us!' But he will reply, 'I do not know you.' ²⁶ You will say, 'But we ate and drank with you, and you taught in our streets.' ²⁷ And he will reply, 'I tell you, I don't know you. Go away, all you who do evil.'
²⁸ "And there will be great weeping and gnashing of teeth, for you will see Abraham, Isaac, Jacob, and all the prophets within the Kingdom of God, but you will be

thrown out. ²⁹ Then people will come from all over the world to take their places in the Kingdom of God. ³⁰ And note this: Some who are despised now will be greatly honoured then; and some who are greatly honoured now will be despised then.*"

Jesus Grieves over Jerusalem

³¹ A few minutes later some Pharisees said to him, "Get out of here if you want to live, because Herod Antipas wants to kill you!"

³² Jesus replied, "Go tell that fox that I will keep on casting out demons and doing miracles of healing today and tomorrow; and the third day I will accomplish my purpose. ³³ Yes, today, tomorrow, and the next day I must proceed on my way. For it wouldn't do for a prophet of God to be killed except in Jerusalem!

³⁴ "O Jerusalem, Jerusalem, the city that kills the prophets and stones God's messengers! How often I have wanted to gather your children together as a hen protects her chicks beneath her wings, but you wouldn't let me. ³⁵ And now look, your house is left to you empty. And you will never see me again until you say, 'Bless the one who comes in the name of the Lord!'*"

CHAPTER 14

Jesus Heals on the Sabbath

One Sabbath day Jesus was in the home of a leader of the Pharisees. The people were watching him closely, ² because there was a man there whose arms and legs were swollen.* ³ Jesus asked the Pharisees and experts in religious law, "Well, is it permitted in the law to heal people on the Sabbath day, or not?" ⁴ When they refused to answer, Jesus touched the sick man and healed him and sent him away. ⁵ Then he turned to them and asked, "Which of you doesn't work on the Sabbath? If your son* or your cow falls into a pit, don't you proceed at once to get him out?" ⁶ Again they had no answer.

Jesus Teaches about Humility

⁷ When Jesus noticed that all who had come to the dinner were trying to sit near the head of the table, he gave them this advice: ⁸ "If you are invited to a wedding feast, don't always head for the best seat. What if someone more respected than you has also been invited? ⁹ The host will say, 'Let this person sit here instead.' Then you will be embarrassed and will have to take whatever seat is left at the foot of the table!

¹⁰ "Do this instead—sit at the foot of the table. Then when your host sees you, he will come and say, 'Friend, we have a better place than this for you!' Then you will be honoured in front of all the other guests. ¹¹ For the proud will be humbled, but the humble will be honoured."

¹² Then he turned to his host. "When you put on a luncheon or a dinner," he said, "don't invite your friends, brothers, relatives, and rich neighbours. For they will repay you by inviting you back. ¹³ Instead, invite the poor, the crippled, the lame, and the blind. ¹⁴ Then at the resurrection of the godly, God will reward you for inviting those who could not repay you."

Story of the Great Feast

¹⁵ Hearing this, a man sitting at the table with Jesus exclaimed, "What a privilege it would be to have a share in the Kingdom of God!"

¹⁶ Jesus replied with this illustration: "A man prepared a great feast and sent out many invitations. ¹⁷ When all was ready, he sent his servant around to notify the guests that it was time for them to come. ¹⁸ But they all began making excuses. One said he had just bought a field and wanted to inspect it, so he asked to be excused.

¹⁹ Another said he had just bought five pair of oxen and wanted to try them out. ²⁰ Another had just been married, so he said he couldn't come.

²¹ "The servant returned and told his master what they had said. His master was angry and said, 'Go quickly into the streets and alleys of the city and invite the poor, the crippled, the lame, and the blind.' ²² After the servant had done this, he reported, 'There is still room for more.' ²³ So his master said, 'Go out into the country lanes and behind the hedges and urge anyone you find to come, so that the house will be full. ²⁴ For none of those I invited first will get even the smallest taste of what I had prepared for them.'"

The Cost of Being a Disciple

²⁵ Great crowds were following Jesus. He turned around and said to them, ²⁶ "If you want to be my follower you must love me more than* your own father and mother, wife and children, brothers and sisters—yes, more than your own life. Otherwise, you cannot be my disciple. ²⁷ And you cannot be my disciple if you do not carry your own cross and follow me.

²⁸ "But don't begin until you count the cost. For who would begin construction of a building without first getting estimates and then checking to see if there is enough money to pay the bills? ²⁹ Otherwise, you might complete only the foundation before running out of funds. And then how everyone would laugh at you! ³⁰ They would say, 'There's the person who started that building and ran out of money before it was finished!'

³¹ "Or what king would ever dream of going to war without first sitting down with his counsellors and discussing whether his army of ten thousand is strong enough to defeat the twenty thousand soldiers who are marching against him? ³² If he is not able, then while the enemy is still far away, he will send a delegation to discuss terms of peace. ³³ So no one can become my disciple without giving up everything for me.

³⁴ "Salt is good for seasoning. But if it loses its flavour, how do you make it salty again? ³⁵ Flavourless salt is good neither for the soil nor for fertilizer. It is thrown away. Anyone who is willing to hear should listen and understand!"

CHAPTER 15

Story of the Lost Sheep

Tax collectors and other notorious sinners often came to listen to Jesus teach. ² This made the Pharisees and teachers of religious law complain that he was associating with such despicable people—even eating with them!

³ So Jesus used this illustration: ⁴ "If you had one hundred sheep, and one of them strayed away and was lost in the

wilderness, wouldn't you leave the ninety-nine others to go and search for the lost one until you found it? ⁵And then you would joyfully carry it home on your shoulders. ⁶When you arrived, you would call together your friends and neighbours to rejoice with you because your lost sheep was found. ⁷In the same way, heaven will be happier over one lost sinner who returns to God than over ninety-nine others who are righteous and haven't strayed away!

Story of the Lost Coin

⁸"Or suppose a woman has ten valuable silver coins* and loses one. Won't she light a lamp and look in every corner of the house and sweep every nook and cranny until she finds it? ⁹And when she finds it, she will call in her friends and neighbours to rejoice with her because she has found her lost coin. ¹⁰In the same way, there is joy in the presence of God's angels when even one sinner repents."

Story of the Lost Son

¹¹To illustrate the point further, Jesus told them this story: "A man had two sons. ¹²The younger son told his father, 'I want my share of your estate now, instead of waiting until you die.' So his father agreed to divide his wealth between his sons.

¹³"A few days later this younger son packed all his belongings and took a trip to a distant land, and there he wasted all his money on wild living. ¹⁴About the time his money ran out, a great famine swept over the land, and he began to starve. ¹⁵He persuaded a local farmer to hire him to feed his pigs. ¹⁶The boy became so hungry that

even the pods he was feeding the pigs looked good to him. But no one gave him anything.

¹⁷ "When he finally came to his senses, he said to himself, 'At home even the hired men have food enough to spare, and here I am, dying of hunger! ¹⁸ I will go home to my father and say, "Father, I have sinned against both heaven and you, ¹⁹ and I am no longer worthy of being called your son. Please take me on as a hired man." '

²⁰ "So he returned home to his father. And while he was still a long distance away, his father saw him coming. Filled with love and compassion, he ran to his son, embraced him, and kissed him. ²¹ His son said to him, 'Father, I have sinned against both heaven and you, and I am no longer worthy of being called your son.'"

²² "But his father said to the servants, 'Quick! Bring the finest robe in the house and put it on him. Get a ring for his finger, and sandals for his feet. ²³ And kill the calf we have been fattening in the pen. We must celebrate with a feast, ²⁴ for this son of mine was dead and has now returned to life. He was lost, but now he is found.' So the party began.

²⁵ "Meanwhile, the older son was in the fields working. When he returned home, he heard music and dancing in the house, ²⁶ and he asked one of the servants what was going on. ²⁷ 'Your brother is back,' he was told, 'and your father has killed the calf we were fattening and has prepared a great feast. We are celebrating because of his safe return.'

²⁸ "The older brother was angry and wouldn't go in. His father came out and begged him, ²⁹ but he replied, 'All these years I've worked hard for you and never once refused to do a single thing you told me to. And in all

that time you never gave me even one young goat for a feast with my friends. [30] Yet when this son of yours comes back after squandering your money on prostitutes, you celebrate by killing the finest calf we have.'

[31] "His father said to him, 'Look, dear son, you and I are very close, and everything I have is yours. [32] We had to celebrate this happy day. For your brother was dead and has come back to life! He was lost, but now he is found!' "

CHAPTER 16

Story of the Shrewd Manager

Jesus told this story to his disciples: "A rich man hired a manager to handle his affairs, but soon a rumour went around that the manager was thoroughly dishonest. [2] So his employer called him in and said, 'What's this I hear about your stealing from me? Get your report in order, because you are going to be dismissed.'

[3] "The manager thought to himself, 'Now what? I'm finished here, and I don't have the strength to go out and dig ditches, and I'm too proud to beg. [4] I know just the thing! Then I'll have plenty of friends to take care of me when I leave!'

[5] "So he invited each person who owed money to his employer to come and discuss the situation. He asked the first one, 'How much do you owe him?' [6] The man replied, 'I owe him eight hundred measures of olive oil.' So the manager told him, 'Tear up that bill and write another one for four hundred measures.'

[7] " 'And how much do you owe my employer?' he asked the next man. 'A thousand measures of wheat,' was the

reply. 'Here,' the manager said, 'take your bill and replace it with one for only eight hundred measures.'"

⁸ "The rich man had to admire the dishonest rascal for being so shrewd. And it is true that the citizens of this world are more shrewd than the godly are. ⁹ I tell you, use your worldly resources to benefit others and make friends. In this way, your generosity stores up a reward for you in heaven.*

¹⁰ "Unless you are faithful in small matters, you won't be faithful in large ones. If you cheat even a little, you won't be honest with greater responsibilities. ¹¹ And if you are untrustworthy about worldly wealth, who will trust you with the true riches of heaven? ¹² And if you are not faithful with other people's money, why should you be trusted with money of your own?

¹³ "No one can serve two masters. For you will hate one and love the other, or be devoted to one and despise the other. You cannot serve both God and money."

¹⁴ The Pharisees, who dearly loved their money, naturally scoffed at all this. ¹⁵ Then he said to them, "You like to look good in public, but God knows your evil hearts. What this world honours is an abomination in the sight of God.

¹⁶ "Until John the Baptist began to preach, the laws of Moses and the messages of the prophets were your guides. But now the Good News of the Kingdom of God is preached, and eager multitudes are forcing their way in. ¹⁷ But that doesn't mean that the law has lost its force in even the smallest point. It is stronger and more permanent than heaven and earth.

18 "Anyone who divorces his wife and marries someone else commits adultery, and anyone who marries a divorced woman commits adultery."

The Rich Man and Lazarus

19 Jesus said, "There was a certain rich man who was splendidly clothed and who lived each day in luxury. 20 At his door lay a diseased beggar named Lazarus. 21 As Lazarus lay there longing for scraps from the rich man's table, the dogs would come and lick his open sores. 22 Finally, the beggar died and was carried by the angels to be with Abraham.* The rich man also died and was buried, 23 and his soul went to the place of the dead.* There, in torment, he saw Lazarus in the far distance with Abraham.

24 "The rich man shouted, 'Father Abraham, have some pity! Send Lazarus over here to dip the tip of his finger in water and cool my tongue, because I am in anguish in these flames.'

25 "But Abraham said to him, 'Son, remember that during your lifetime you had everything you wanted, and Lazarus had nothing. So now he is here being comforted, and you are in anguish. 26 And besides, there is a great chasm separating us. Anyone who wants to cross over to you from here is stopped at its edge, and no one there can cross over to us.'

27 "Then the rich man said, 'Please, Father Abraham, send him to my father's home. 28 For I have five brothers, and I want him to warn them about this place of torment so they won't have to come here when they die.'

29 "But Abraham said, 'Moses and the prophets have warned them. Your brothers can read their writings any time they want to.'

³⁰ "The rich man replied, 'No, Father Abraham! But if someone is sent to them from the dead, then they will turn from their sins.'

³¹ "But Abraham said, 'If they won't listen to Moses and the prophets, they won't listen even if someone rises from the dead.'"

CHAPTER 17

Teachings about Forgiveness and Faith

One day Jesus said to his disciples, "There will always be temptations to sin, but how terrible it will be for the person who does the tempting. ² It would be better to be thrown into the sea with a large millstone tied around the neck than to face the punishment in store for harming one of these little ones. ³ I am warning you! If another believer* sins, rebuke him; then if he repents, forgive him. ⁴ Even if he wrongs you seven times a day and each time turns again and asks forgiveness, forgive him."

⁵ One day the apostles said to the Lord, "We need more faith; tell us how to get it."

⁶ "Even if you had faith as small as a mustard seed," the Lord answered, "you could say to this mulberry tree, 'May God uproot you and throw you into the sea,' and it would obey you!

⁷ "When a servant comes in from ploughing or looking after the sheep, he doesn't just sit down and eat. ⁸ He must first prepare his master's meal and serve him his supper before eating his own. ⁹ And the servant is not even thanked, because he is merely doing what he is supposed to do. ¹⁰ In the same way, when you obey me

you should say, 'We are not worthy of praise. We are servants who have simply done our duty.' "

Ten Healed of Leprosy

[11] As Jesus continued on towards Jerusalem, he reached the border between Galilee and Samaria. [12] As he entered a village there, ten lepers stood at a distance, [13] crying out, "Jesus, Master, have mercy on us!"

[14] He looked at them and said, "Go and show yourselves to the priests." And as they went, their leprosy disappeared.

[15] One of them, when he saw that he was healed, came back to Jesus, shouting, "Praise God, I'm healed!" [16] He fell face down on the ground at Jesus' feet, thanking him for what he had done. This man was a Samaritan.

[17] Jesus asked, "Didn't I heal ten men? Where are the other nine? [18] Does only this foreigner return to give glory to God?" [19] And Jesus said to the man, "Stand up and go. Your faith has made you well."

The Coming of the Kingdom

[20] One day the Pharisees asked Jesus, "When will the Kingdom of God come?"

Jesus replied, "The Kingdom of God isn't ushered in with visible signs.* [21] You won't be able to say, 'Here it is!' or 'It's over there!' For the Kingdom of God is among you.*"

[22] Later he talked again about this with his disciples. "The time is coming when you will long to share in the days of the Son of Man, but you won't be able to," he said. [23] "Reports will reach you that the Son of Man has returned and that he is in this place or that. Don't believe

such reports or go out to look for him. ²⁴For when the Son of Man returns, you will know it beyond all doubt. It will be as evident as the lightning that flashes across the sky. ²⁵But first the Son of Man must suffer terribly* and be rejected by this generation.

²⁶"When the Son of Man returns, the world will be like the people were in Noah's day. ²⁷In those days before the flood, the people enjoyed banquets and parties and weddings right up to the time Noah entered his boat and the flood came to destroy them all.

²⁸"And the world will be as it was in the days of Lot. People went about their daily business—eating and drinking, buying and selling, farming and building—²⁹until the morning Lot left Sodom. Then fire and burning sulphur rained down from heaven and destroyed them all. ³⁰Yes, it will be 'business as usual' right up to the hour when the Son of Man returns.* ³¹On that day a person outside the house* must not go into the house to pack. A person in the field must not return to town. ³²Remember what happened to Lot's wife! ³³Whoever clings to this life will lose it, and whoever loses this life will save it. ³⁴That night two people will be asleep in one bed; one will be taken away, and the other will be left. ³⁵Two women will be grinding flour together at the mill; one will be taken, the other left.*"

³⁷"Lord, where will this happen?" the disciples asked.

Jesus replied, "Just as the gathering of vultures shows there is a carcass nearby, so these signs indicate that the end is near."*

CHAPTER 18

Story of the Persistent Widow

One day Jesus told his disciples a story to illustrate their need for constant prayer and to show them that they must never give up. ²"There was a judge in a certain city," he said, "who was a godless man with great contempt for everyone. ³A widow of that city came to him repeatedly, appealing for justice against someone who had harmed her. ⁴The judge ignored her for a while, but eventually she wore him out. 'I fear neither God nor man,' he said to himself, ⁵'but this woman is driving me crazy. I'm going to see that she gets justice, because she is wearing me out with her constant requests!'"

⁶Then the Lord said, "Learn a lesson from this evil judge. ⁷Even he rendered a just decision in the end, so don't you think God will surely give justice to his chosen people who plead with him day and night? Will he keep putting them off? ⁸I tell you, he will grant justice to them quickly! But when I, the Son of Man, return, how many will I find who have faith?"

Story of the Pharisee and Tax Collector

⁹Then Jesus told this story to some who had great self-confidence and scorned everyone else: ¹⁰"Two men went to the Temple to pray. One was a Pharisee, and the other was a dishonest tax collector. ¹¹The proud Pharisee stood by himself and prayed this prayer: 'I thank you, God, that I am not a sinner like everyone else, especially like that tax collector over there! For I never cheat, I don't

sin, I don't commit adultery, ¹²I fast twice a week, and I give you a tenth of my income.'

¹³"But the tax collector stood at a distance and dared not even lift his eyes to heaven as he prayed. Instead, he beat his chest in sorrow, saying, 'O God, be merciful to me, for I am a sinner.' ¹⁴I tell you, this sinner, not the Pharisee, returned home justified before God. For the proud will be humbled, but the humble will be honoured."

Jesus Blesses the Children

¹⁵One day some parents brought their little children to Jesus so he could touch them and bless them, but the disciples told them not to bother him. ¹⁶Then Jesus called for the children and said to the disciples, "Let the children come to me. Don't stop them! For the Kingdom of God belongs to such as these. ¹⁷I assure you, anyone who doesn't have their kind of faith will never get into the Kingdom of God."

The Rich Man

¹⁸Once a religious leader asked Jesus this question: "Good teacher, what should I do to get eternal life?"

¹⁹"Why do you call me good?" Jesus asked him. "Only God is truly good. ²⁰But as for your question, you know the commandments: 'Do not commit adultery. Do not murder. Do not steal. Do not testify falsely. Honour your father and mother.'* "

²¹The man replied, "I've obeyed all these commandments since I was a child."

²²"There is still one thing you lack," Jesus said. "Sell all you have and give the money to the poor, and you will

have treasure in heaven. Then come, follow me." ²³ But when the man heard this, he became sad because he was very rich.

²⁴ Jesus watched him go and then said to his disciples, "How hard it is for rich people to get into the Kingdom of God! ²⁵ It is easier for a camel to go through the eye of a needle than for a rich person to enter the Kingdom of God!"

²⁶ Those who heard this said, "Then who in the world can be saved?"

²⁷ He replied, "What is impossible from a human perspective is possible with God."

²⁸ Peter said, "We have left our homes and followed you."

²⁹ "Yes," Jesus replied, "and I assure you, everyone who has given up house or wife or brothers or parents or children, for the sake of the Kingdom of God, ³⁰ will be repaid many times over in this life, as well as receiving eternal life in the world to come."

Jesus Again Predicts His Death

³¹ Gathering the twelve disciples around him, Jesus told them, "As you know, we are going to Jerusalem. And when we get there, all the predictions of the ancient prophets concerning the Son of Man will come true. ³² He will be handed over to the Romans to be mocked, treated shamefully, and spit upon. ³³ They will whip him and kill him, but on the third day he will rise again."

³⁴ But they didn't understand a thing he said. Its significance was hidden from them, and they failed to grasp what he was talking about.

Jesus Heals a Blind Beggar

³⁵ As they approached Jericho, a blind beggar was sitting beside the road. ³⁶ When he heard the noise of a crowd going past, he asked what was happening. ³⁷ They told him that Jesus of Nazareth was going by. ³⁸ So he began shouting, "Jesus, Son of David, have mercy on me!" ³⁹ The crowds ahead of Jesus tried to hush the man, but he only shouted louder, "Son of David, have mercy on me!"

⁴⁰ When Jesus heard him, he stopped and ordered that the man be brought to him. ⁴¹ Then Jesus asked the man, "What do you want me to do for you?"

"Lord," he pleaded, "I want to see!"

⁴² And Jesus said, "All right, you can see! Your faith has healed you." ⁴³ Instantly the man could see, and he followed Jesus, praising God. And all who saw it praised God, too.

CHAPTER 19

Jesus and Zacchaeus

Jesus entered Jericho and made his way through the town. ² There was a man there named Zacchaeus. He was one of the most influential Jews in the Roman tax-collecting business, and he had become very rich. ³ He tried to get a look at Jesus, but he was too short to see over the crowds. ⁴ So he ran ahead and climbed a sycamore tree beside the road, so he could watch from there.

⁵ When Jesus came by, he looked up at Zacchaeus and called him by name. "Zacchaeus!" he said. "Quick, come down! For I must be a guest in your home today."

⁶Zacchaeus quickly climbed down and took Jesus to his house in great excitement and joy. ⁷But the crowds were displeased. "He has gone to be the guest of a notorious sinner," they grumbled.

⁸Meanwhile, Zacchaeus stood there and said to the Lord, "I will give half my wealth to the poor, Lord, and if I have overcharged people on their taxes, I will give them back four times as much!"

⁹Jesus responded, "Salvation has come to this home today, for this man has shown himself to be a son of Abraham. ¹⁰And I, the Son of Man, have come to seek and save those like him who are lost."

Story of the Ten Servants

¹¹The crowd was listening to everything Jesus said. And because he was nearing Jerusalem, he told a story to correct the impression that the Kingdom of God would begin right away. ¹²He said, "A nobleman was called away to a distant empire to be crowned king and then return. ¹³Before he left, he called together ten servants and gave them a small fortune in silver* to invest for him while he was gone. ¹⁴But his people hated him and sent a delegation after him to say they did not want him to be their king.

¹⁵"When he returned, the king called in the servants to whom he had given the money. He wanted to find out what they had done with the money and what their profits were. ¹⁶The first servant reported a tremendous gain—ten times as much as the original amount! ¹⁷'Well done!' the king exclaimed. 'You are a trustworthy servant. You have been faithful with the little I entrusted to you, so you will be governor of ten cities as your reward.'

¹⁸ "The next servant also reported a good gain—five times the original amount. ¹⁹ 'Well done!' the king said. 'You can be governor over five cities.'

²⁰ "But the third servant brought back only the original amount of money and said, 'I hid it and kept it safe. ²¹ I was afraid because you are a hard man to deal with, taking what isn't yours and harvesting crops you didn't plant.'

²² " 'You wicked servant!' the king roared. 'Hard, am I? If you knew so much about me and how tough I am, ²³ why didn't you deposit the money in the bank so I could at least get some interest on it?' ²⁴ Then turning to the others standing nearby, the king ordered, 'Take the money from this servant, and give it to the one who earned the most.'

²⁵ " 'But, master,' they said, 'that servant has enough already!'

²⁶ " 'Yes,' the king replied, 'but to those who use well what they are given, even more will be given. But from those who are unfaithful,* even what little they have will be taken away. ²⁷ And now about these enemies of mine who didn't want me to be their king—bring them in and execute them right here in my presence.' "

The Triumphal Entry

²⁸ After telling this story, Jesus went on towards Jerusalem, walking ahead of his disciples. ²⁹ As they came to the towns of Bethphage and Bethany, on the Mount of Olives, he sent two disciples ahead. ³⁰ "Go into that village over there," he told them, "and as you enter it, you will see a colt tied there that has never been ridden. Untie it and bring it here. ³¹ If anyone asks what you are doing, just say, 'The Lord needs it.' "

³² So they went and found the colt, just as Jesus had said. ³³ And sure enough, as they were untying it, the owners asked them, "Why are you untying our colt?"

³⁴ And the disciples simply replied, "The Lord needs it." ³⁵ So they brought the colt to Jesus and threw their garments over it for him to ride on.

³⁶ Then the crowds spread out their coats on the road ahead of Jesus. ³⁷ As they reached the place where the road started down from the Mount of Olives, all of his followers began to shout and sing as they walked along, praising God for all the wonderful miracles they had seen.

³⁸ "Bless the King who comes in the name of the Lord!
  Peace in heaven
     and glory in highest heaven!"*

³⁹ But some of the Pharisees among the crowd said, "Teacher, rebuke your followers for saying things like that!"

⁴⁰ He replied, "If they kept quiet, the stones along the road would burst into cheers!"

Jesus Weeps over Jerusalem

⁴¹ But as they came closer to Jerusalem and Jesus saw the city ahead, he began to weep. ⁴² "I wish that even today you would find the way of peace. But now it is too late, and peace is hidden from you. ⁴³ Before long your enemies will build ramparts against your walls and encircle you and close in on you. ⁴⁴ They will crush you to the ground, and your children with you. Your enemies will not leave a single stone in place, because you have rejected the opportunity God offered you."

Jesus Clears the Temple

⁴⁵ Then Jesus entered the Temple and began to drive out the merchants from their stalls. ⁴⁶ He told them, "The Scriptures declare, 'My Temple will be a place of prayer,' but you have turned it into a den of thieves.'"*

⁴⁷ After that, he taught daily in the Temple, but the leading priests, the teachers of religious law, and the other leaders of the people began planning how to kill him. ⁴⁸ But they could think of nothing, because all the people hung on every word he said.

CHAPTER 20

The Authority of Jesus Challenged

One day as Jesus was teaching and preaching the Good News in the Temple, the leading priests and teachers of religious law and other leaders came up to him. ² They demanded, "By whose authority did you drive out the merchants from the Temple?* Who gave you such authority?"

³ "Let me ask you a question first," he replied. ⁴ "Did John's baptism come from heaven, or was it merely human?"

⁵ They talked it over among themselves. "If we say it was from heaven, he will ask why we didn't believe him. ⁶ But if we say it was merely human, the people will stone us, because they are convinced he was a prophet." ⁷ Finally they replied, "We don't know."

⁸ And Jesus responded, "Then I won't answer your question either."

Story of the Evil Farmers

⁹Now Jesus turned to the people again and told them this story: "A man planted a vineyard, leased it out to tenant farmers, and moved to another country to live for several years. ¹⁰At grape-picking time, he sent one of his servants to collect his share of the crop. But the farmers attacked the servant, beat him up, and sent him back empty-handed. ¹¹So the owner sent another servant, but the same thing happened; he was beaten up and treated shamefully, and he went away empty-handed. ¹²A third man was sent and the same thing happened. He, too, was wounded and chased away.

¹³" 'What will I do?' the owner asked himself. 'I know! I'll send my cherished son. Surely they will respect him.'

¹⁴"But when the farmers saw his son, they said to each other, 'Here comes the heir to this estate. Let's kill him and get the estate for ourselves!' ¹⁵So they dragged him out of the vineyard and murdered him.

"What do you suppose the owner of the vineyard will do to those farmers?" Jesus asked. ¹⁶"I'll tell you—he will come and kill them all and lease the vineyard to others."

"But God forbid that such a thing should ever happen," his listeners protested.

¹⁷Jesus looked at them and said, "Then what do the Scriptures mean?

'The stone rejected by the builders
    has now become the cornerstone.'*
¹⁸All who stumble over that stone will be broken to pieces, and it will crush anyone on whom it falls."

¹⁹When the teachers of religious law and the leading priests heard this story, they wanted to arrest Jesus immediately because they realized he was pointing at

them—that they were the farmers in the story. But they were afraid there would be a riot if they arrested him.

Taxes for Caesar

[20] Watching for their opportunity, the leaders sent secret agents pretending to be honest men. They tried to get Jesus to say something that could be reported to the Roman governor so he would arrest Jesus. [21] They said, "Teacher, we know that you speak and teach what is right and are not influenced by what others think. You sincerely teach the ways of God. [22] Now tell us—is it right to pay taxes to the Roman government or not?"

[23] He saw through their trickery and said, [24] "Show me a Roman coin.* Whose picture and title are stamped on it?"

"Caesar's," they replied.

[25] "Well then," he said, "give to Caesar what belongs to him. But everything that belongs to God must be given to God." [26] So they failed to trap him in the presence of the people. Instead, they were amazed by his answer, and they were silenced.

Discussion about Resurrection

[27] Then some Sadducees stepped forward—a group of Jews who say there is no resurrection after death. [28] They posed this question: "Teacher, Moses gave us a law that if a man dies, leaving a wife but no children, his brother should marry the widow and have a child who will be the brother's heir.* [29] Well, there were seven brothers. The oldest married and then died without children. [30] His brother married the widow, but he also died. Still no children. [31] And so it went, one after the other, until each

of the seven had married her and died, leaving no children. ³²Finally, the woman died, too. ³³So tell us, whose wife will she be in the resurrection? For all seven were married to her!"

³⁴Jesus replied, "Marriage is for people here on earth. ³⁵But that is not the way it will be in the age to come. For those worthy of being raised from the dead won't be married then. ³⁶And they will never die again. In these respects they are like angels. They are children of God raised up to new life. ³⁷But now, as to whether the dead will be raised—even Moses proved this when he wrote about the burning bush. Long after Abraham, Isaac, and Jacob had died, he referred to the Lord*ᵃ as 'the God of Abraham, the God of Isaac, and the God of Jacob.'*ᵇ ³⁸So he is the God of the living, not the dead. They are all alive to him."

³⁹"Well said, Teacher!" remarked some of the teachers of religious law who were standing there. ⁴⁰And that ended their questions; no one dared to ask any more.

Whose Son Is the Messiah?

⁴¹Then Jesus presented them with a question. "Why is it," he asked, "that the Messiah is said to be the son of David? ⁴²For David himself wrote in the book of Psalms:

'The LORD said to my Lord,
  Sit in honour at my right hand
⁴³   until I humble your enemies,
      making them a footstool under your feet.'*

⁴⁴Since David called him Lord, how can he be his son at the same time?"

⁴⁵Then, with the crowds listening, he turned to his disciples and said, ⁴⁶"Beware of these teachers of

religious law! For they love to parade in flowing robes and to have everyone bow to them as they walk in the marketplaces. And how they love the seats of honour in the synagogues and at banquets. ⁴⁷ But they shamelessly cheat widows out of their property, and then, to cover up the kind of people they really are, they make long prayers in public. Because of this, their punishment will be the greater."

CHAPTER 21

The Widow's Offering

While Jesus was in the Temple, he watched the rich people putting their gifts into the collection box. ²Then a poor widow came by and dropped in two pennies.* ³"I assure you," he said, "this poor widow has given more than all the rest of them. ⁴For they have given a tiny part of their surplus, but she, poor as she is, has given everything she has."

Jesus Foretells the Future

⁵ Some of his disciples began talking about the beautiful stonework of the Temple and the memorial decorations on the walls. But Jesus said, ⁶"The time is coming when all these things will be so completely demolished that not one stone will be left on top of another."

⁷ "Teacher," they asked, "when will all this take place? And will there be any sign ahead of time?"

⁸ He replied, "Don't let anyone mislead you. For many will come in my name, claiming to be the Messiah* and saying, 'The time has come!' But don't believe them.

⁹ And when you hear of wars and insurrections, don't panic. Yes, these things must come, but the end won't follow immediately." ¹⁰ Then he added, "Nations and kingdoms will proclaim war against each other. ¹¹ There will be great earthquakes, and there will be famines and epidemics in many lands, and there will be terrifying things and great miraculous signs in the heavens.

¹² "But before all this occurs, there will be a time of great persecution. You will be dragged into synagogues and prisons, and you will be accused before kings and governors of being my followers. ¹³ This will be your opportunity to tell them about me. ¹⁴ So don't worry about how to answer the charges against you, ¹⁵ for I will give you the right words and such wisdom that none of your opponents will be able to reply! ¹⁶ Even those closest to you—your parents, brothers, relatives, and friends—will betray you. And some of you will be killed. ¹⁷ And everyone will hate you because of your allegiance to me. ¹⁸ But not a hair of your head will perish! ¹⁹ By standing firm, you will win your souls.

²⁰ "And when you see Jerusalem surrounded by armies, then you will know that the time of its destruction has arrived. ²¹ Then those in Judea must flee to the hills. Let those in Jerusalem escape, and those outside the city should not enter it for shelter. ²² For those will be days of God's vengeance, and the prophetic words of the Scriptures will be fulfilled. ²³ How terrible it will be for pregnant women and for mothers nursing their babies. For there will be great distress in the land and wrath upon this people. ²⁴ They will be brutally killed by the sword or sent away as captives to all the nations of the world. And

Jerusalem will be conquered and trampled down by the Gentiles until the age of the Gentiles comes to an end.

²⁵ "And there will be strange events in the skies—signs in the sun, moon, and stars. And down here on earth the nations will be in turmoil, perplexed by the roaring seas and strange tides. ²⁶ The courage of many people will falter because of the fearful fate they see coming upon the earth, because the stability of the very heavens will be broken up. ²⁷ Then everyone will see the Son of Man arrive on the clouds with power and great glory.* ²⁸ So when all these things begin to happen, stand straight and look up, for your salvation is near!"

²⁹ Then he gave them this illustration: "Notice the fig tree, or any other tree. ³⁰ When the leaves come out, you know without being told that summer is near. ³¹ Just so, when you see the events I've described taking place, you can be sure that the Kingdom of God is near. ³² I assure you, this generation* will not pass from the scene until all these events have taken place. ³³ Heaven and earth will disappear, but my words will remain for ever.

³⁴ "Watch out! Don't let me find you living in careless ease and drunkenness, and filled with the worries of this life. Don't let that day catch you unaware, ³⁵ as in a trap. For that day will come upon everyone living on the earth. ³⁶ Keep a constant watch. And pray that, if possible, you may escape these horrors and stand before the Son of Man."

³⁷ Every day Jesus went to the Temple to teach, and each evening he returned to spend the night on the Mount of Olives. ³⁸ The crowds gathered early each morning to hear him.

CHAPTER 22

Judas Agrees to Betray Jesus

The Festival of Unleavened Bread, which begins with the Passover celebration, was drawing near. ²The leading priests and teachers of religious law were actively plotting Jesus' murder. But they wanted to kill him without starting a riot, a possibility they greatly feared.

³Then Satan entered into Judas Iscariot, who was one of the twelve disciples, ⁴and he went over to the leading priests and captains of the Temple guard to discuss the best way to betray Jesus to them. ⁵They were delighted that he was ready to help them, and they promised him a reward. ⁶So he began looking for an opportunity to betray Jesus so they could arrest him quietly when the crowds weren't around.

The Last Supper

⁷Now the Festival of Unleavened Bread arrived, when the Passover lambs were sacrificed. ⁸Jesus sent Peter and John ahead and said, "Go and prepare the Passover meal, so we can eat it together."

⁹"Where do you want us to go?" they asked him.

¹⁰He replied, "As soon as you enter Jerusalem, a man carrying a pitcher of water will meet you. Follow him. At the house he enters, ¹¹say to the owner, 'The Teacher asks: Where is the guest room where I can eat the Passover meal with my disciples?' ¹²He will take you upstairs to a large room that is already set up. That is the place. Go ahead and prepare our supper there." ¹³They

went off to the city and found everything just as Jesus had said, and they prepared the Passover supper there.

[14] Then at the proper time Jesus and the twelve apostles sat down together at the table. [15] Jesus said, "I have looked forward to this hour with deep longing, anxious to eat this Passover meal with you before my suffering begins. [16] For I tell you now that I won't eat it again until it comes to fulfilment in the Kingdom of God."

[17] Then he took a cup of wine, and when he had given thanks for it, he said, "Take this and share it among yourselves. [18] For I will not drink wine again until the Kingdom of God has come."

[19] Then he took a loaf of bread; and when he had thanked God for it, he broke it in pieces and gave it to the disciples, saying, "This is my body, given for you. Do this in remembrance of me." [20] After supper he took another cup of wine and said, "This wine is the token of God's new covenant to save you—an agreement sealed with the blood I will pour out for you.*

[21] "But here at this table, sitting among us as a friend, is the man who will betray me. [22] For I, the Son of Man, must die since it is part of God's plan. But how terrible it will be for my betrayer!" [23] Then the disciples began to ask each other which of them would ever do such a thing.

[24] And they began to argue among themselves as to who would be the greatest in the coming Kingdom. [25] Jesus told them, "In this world the kings and great men order their people around, and yet they are called 'friends of the people.' [26] But among you, those who are the greatest should take the lowest rank, and the leader should be like a servant. [27] Normally the master sits at the table and is served by his servants. But not here! For I

am your servant. ²⁸You have remained true to me in my time of trial. ²⁹And just as my Father has granted me a Kingdom, I now grant you the right ³⁰to eat and drink at my table in that Kingdom. And you will sit on thrones, judging the twelve tribes of Israel.

Jesus Predicts Peter's Denial

³¹"Simon, Simon, Satan has asked to have all of you, to sift you like wheat. ³²But I have pleaded in prayer for you, Simon, that your faith should not fail. So when you have repented and turned to me again, strengthen and build up your brothers."

³³Peter said, "Lord, I am ready to go to prison with you, and even to die with you."

³⁴But Jesus said, "Peter, let me tell you something. The cock will not crow tomorrow morning until you have denied three times that you even know me."

³⁵Then Jesus asked them, "When I sent you out to preach the Good News and you did not have money, a traveller's bag, or extra clothing, did you lack anything?"

"No," they replied.

³⁶"But now," he said, "take your money and a traveller's bag. And if you don't have a sword, sell your clothes and buy one! ³⁷For the time has come for this prophecy about me to be fulfilled: 'He was counted among those who were rebels.'* Yes, everything written about me by the prophets will come true."

³⁸"Lord," they replied, "we have two swords among us."

"That's enough," he said.

Jesus Prays on the Mount of Olives

³⁹ Then, accompanied by the disciples, Jesus left the upstairs room and went as usual to the Mount of Olives. ⁴⁰ There he told them, "Pray that you will not be overcome by temptation."

⁴¹ He walked away, about a stone's throw, and knelt down and prayed, ⁴² "Father, if you are willing, please take this cup of suffering away from me. Yet I want your will, not mine." ⁴³ Then an angel from heaven appeared and strengthened him. ⁴⁴ He prayed more fervently, and he was in such agony of spirit that his sweat fell to the ground like great drops of blood.* ⁴⁵ At last he stood up again and returned to the disciples, only to find them asleep, exhausted from grief. ⁴⁶ "Why are you sleeping?" he asked. "Get up and pray. Otherwise temptation will overpower you."

Jesus Is Betrayed and Arrested

⁴⁷ But even as he said this, a mob approached, led by Judas, one of his twelve disciples. Judas walked over to Jesus and greeted him with a kiss. ⁴⁸ But Jesus said, "Judas, how can you betray me, the Son of Man, with a kiss?"

⁴⁹ When the other disciples saw what was about to happen, they exclaimed, "Lord, should we fight? We brought the swords!" ⁵⁰ And one of them slashed at the high priest's servant and cut off his right ear.

⁵¹ But Jesus said, "Don't resist any more." And he touched the place where the man's ear had been and healed him. ⁵² Then Jesus spoke to the leading priests and captains of the Temple guard and the other leaders who headed the mob. "Am I some dangerous criminal," he asked, "that you have come armed with swords and clubs

to arrest me? ⁵³ Why didn't you arrest me in the Temple? I was there every day. But this is your moment, the time when the power of darkness reigns."

Peter Denies Jesus

⁵⁴ So they arrested him and led him to the high priest's residence, and Peter was following far behind. ⁵⁵ The guards lit a fire in the courtyard and sat around it, and Peter joined them there. ⁵⁶ A servant girl noticed him in the firelight and began staring at him. Finally she said, "This man was one of Jesus' followers!"

⁵⁷ Peter denied it. "Woman," he said, "I don't even know the man!"

⁵⁸ After a while someone else looked at him and said, "You must be one of that group!"

"No, man, I'm not!" Peter replied.

⁵⁹ About an hour later someone else insisted, "This must be one of Jesus' disciples because he is a Galilean, too."

⁶⁰ But Peter said, "Man, I don't know what you are talking about." And as soon as he said these words, the cock crowed. ⁶¹ At that moment the Lord turned and looked at Peter. Then Peter remembered that the Lord had said, "Before the cock crows tomorrow morning, you will deny me three times." ⁶² And Peter left the courtyard, crying bitterly.

⁶³ Now the guards in charge of Jesus began mocking and beating him. ⁶⁴ They blindfolded him; then they hit him and asked, "Who hit you that time, you prophet?" ⁶⁵ And they threw all sorts of terrible insults at him.

Jesus before the Council

⁶⁶ At daybreak all the leaders of the people assembled, including the leading priests and the teachers of religious law. Jesus was led before this high council,* ⁶⁷ and they said, "Tell us if you are the Messiah."

But he replied, "If I tell you, you won't believe me. ⁶⁸ And if I ask you a question, you won't answer. ⁶⁹ But the time is soon coming when I, the Son of Man, will be sitting at God's right hand in the place of power."*

⁷⁰ They all shouted, "Then you claim you are the Son of God?"

And he replied, "You are right in saying that I am."

⁷¹ "What need do we have for other witnesses?" they shouted. "We ourselves heard him say it."

CHAPTER 23

Jesus' Trial before Pilate

Then the entire council took Jesus over to Pilate, the Roman governor. ² They began at once to state their case: "This man has been leading our people to ruin by telling them not to pay their taxes to the Roman government and by claiming he is the Messiah, a king."

³ So Pilate asked him, "Are you the King of the Jews?"

Jesus replied, "Yes, it is as you say."

⁴ Pilate turned to the leading priests and to the crowd and said, "I find nothing wrong with this man!"

⁵ Then they became desperate. "But he is causing riots everywhere he goes, all over Judea, from Galilee to Jerusalem!"

⁶ "Oh, is he a Galilean?" Pilate asked. ⁷ When they answered that he was, Pilate sent him to Herod Antipas, because Galilee was under Herod's jurisdiction, and Herod happened to be in Jerusalem at the time.

⁸ Herod was delighted at the opportunity to see Jesus, because he had heard about him and had been hoping for a long time to see him perform a miracle. ⁹ He asked Jesus question after question, but Jesus refused to answer. ¹⁰ Meanwhile, the leading priests and the teachers of religious law stood there shouting their accusations. ¹¹ Now Herod and his soldiers began mocking and ridiculing Jesus. Then they put a royal robe on him and sent him back to Pilate. ¹² Herod and Pilate, who had been enemies before, became friends that day.

¹³ Then Pilate called together the leading priests and other religious leaders, along with the people, ¹⁴ and he announced his verdict. "You brought this man to me, accusing him of leading a revolt. I have examined him thoroughly on this point in your presence and find him innocent. ¹⁵ Herod came to the same conclusion and sent him back to us. Nothing this man has done calls for the death penalty. ¹⁶ So I will have him flogged, but then I will release him."*

¹⁸ Then a mighty roar rose from the crowd, and with one voice they shouted, "Kill him, and release Barabbas to us!" ¹⁹ (Barabbas was in prison for murder and for taking part in an insurrection in Jerusalem against the government.) ²⁰ Pilate argued with them, because he wanted to release Jesus. ²¹ But they shouted, "Crucify him! Crucify him!"

²² For the third time he demanded, "Why? What crime has he committed? I have found no reason to sentence him to death. I will therefore flog him and let him go."

²³ But the crowd shouted louder and louder for Jesus' death, and their voices prevailed. ²⁴ So Pilate sentenced Jesus to die as they demanded. ²⁵ As they had requested, he released Barabbas, the man in prison for insurrection and murder. But he delivered Jesus over to them to do as they wished.

The Crucifixion

²⁶ As they led Jesus away, Simon of Cyrene,* who was coming in from the country just then, was forced to follow Jesus and carry his cross. ²⁷ Great crowds trailed along behind, including many grief-stricken women. ²⁸ But Jesus turned and said to them, "Daughters of Jerusalem, don't weep for me, but weep for yourselves and for your children. ²⁹ For the days are coming when they will say, 'Fortunate indeed are the women who are childless, the wombs that have not borne a child and the breasts that have never nursed.' ³⁰ People will beg the mountains to fall on them and the hills to bury them. ³¹ For if these things are done when the tree is green, what will happen when it is dry?*"

³² Two others, both criminals, were led out to be executed with him. ³³ Finally, they came to a place called The Skull.* All three were crucified there—Jesus on the centre cross, and the two criminals on either side.

³⁴ Jesus said, "Father, forgive these people, because they don't know what they are doing."*ᵃ And the soldiers gambled for his clothes by throwing dice.*ᵇ

³⁵ The crowd watched, and the leaders laughed and scoffed. "He saved others," they said, "let him save himself if he is really God's Chosen One, the Messiah."

³⁶ The soldiers mocked him, too, by offering him a drink

of sour wine. ³⁷ They called out to him, "If you are the King of the Jews, save yourself!" ³⁸ A signboard was nailed to the cross above him with these words: "This is the King of the Jews."

³⁹ One of the criminals hanging beside him scoffed, "So you're the Messiah, are you? Prove it by saving yourself—and us, too, while you're at it!"

⁴⁰ But the other criminal protested, "Don't you fear God even when you are dying? ⁴¹ We deserve to die for our evil deeds, but this man hasn't done anything wrong." ⁴² Then he said, "Jesus, remember me when you come into your Kingdom."

⁴³ And Jesus replied, "I assure you, today you will be with me in paradise."

The Death of Jesus

⁴⁴ By this time it was noon, and darkness fell across the whole land until three o'clock. ⁴⁵ The light from the sun was gone. And suddenly, the thick veil hanging in the Temple was torn apart. ⁴⁶ Then Jesus shouted, "Father, I entrust my spirit into your hands!"* And with those words he breathed his last.

⁴⁷ When the captain of the Roman soldiers handling the executions saw what had happened, he praised God and said, "Surely this man was innocent.*" ⁴⁸ And when the crowd that came to see the crucifixion saw all that had happened, they went home in deep sorrow.* ⁴⁹ But Jesus' friends, including the women who had followed him from Galilee, stood at a distance watching.

The Burial of Jesus

⁵⁰ Now there was a good and righteous man named Joseph. He was a member of the Jewish high council, ⁵¹ but he had not agreed with the decision and actions of the other religious leaders. He was from the town of Arimathea in Judea, and he had been waiting for the Kingdom of God to come. ⁵² He went to Pilate and asked for Jesus' body. ⁵³ Then he took the body down from the cross and wrapped it in a long linen cloth and laid it in a new tomb that had been carved out of rock. ⁵⁴ This was done late on Friday afternoon, the day of preparation* for the Sabbath.

⁵⁵ As his body was taken away, the women from Galilee followed and saw the tomb where they placed his body. ⁵⁶ Then they went home and prepared spices and ointments to embalm him. But by the time they were finished it was the Sabbath, so they rested all that day as required by the law.

CHAPTER 24

The Resurrection

But very early on Sunday morning* the women came to the tomb, taking the spices they had prepared. ² They found that the stone covering the entrance had been rolled aside. ³ So they went in, but they couldn't find the body of the Lord Jesus. ⁴ They were puzzled, trying to think what could have happened to it. Suddenly, two men appeared to them, clothed in dazzling robes. ⁵ The women were terrified and bowed low before them. Then the men asked, "Why are you looking in a tomb for someone who is alive? ⁶He isn't here! He has risen from the dead! Don't you remember what he told you back in Galilee, ⁷that the Son of Man must be betrayed into the hands of sinful men and be crucified, and that he would rise again the third day?"

⁸Then they remembered that he had said this. ⁹So they rushed back to tell his eleven disciples—and everyone else—what had happened. ¹⁰The women who went to the tomb were Mary Magdalene, Joanna, Mary the mother of James, and several others. They told the apostles what had happened, ¹¹but the story sounded like nonsense, so they didn't believe it. ¹²However, Peter ran to the tomb to look. Stooping, he peered in and saw the empty linen wrappings; then he went home again, wondering what had happened.*

The Walk to Emmaus

¹³That same day two of Jesus' followers were walking to the village of Emmaus, eleven kilometres* out of Jerusalem. ¹⁴As they walked along they were talking about everything that had happened. ¹⁵Suddenly, Jesus himself came along and joined them and began walking beside them. ¹⁶But they didn't know who he was, because God kept them from recognizing him.

¹⁷"You seem to be in a deep discussion about something," he said. "What are you so concerned about?"

They stopped short, sadness written across their faces. ¹⁸Then one of them, Cleopas, replied, "You must be the only person in Jerusalem who hasn't heard about all the things that have happened there the last few days."

[19]"What things?" Jesus asked.

"The things that happened to Jesus, the man from Nazareth," they said. "He was a prophet who did wonderful miracles. He was a mighty teacher, highly regarded by both God and all the people. [20]But our leading priests and other religious leaders arrested him and handed him over to be condemned to death, and they crucified him. [21]We had thought he was the Messiah who had come to rescue Israel. That all happened three days ago. [22]Then some women from our group of his followers were at his tomb early this morning, and they came back with an amazing report. [23]They said his body was missing, and they had seen angels who told them Jesus is alive! [24]Some of our men ran out to see, and sure enough, Jesus' body was gone, just as the women had said."

[25]Then Jesus said to them, "You are such foolish people! You find it so hard to believe all that the prophets wrote in the Scriptures. [26]Wasn't it clearly predicted by the prophets that the Messiah would have to suffer all these things before entering his time of glory?" [27]Then Jesus quoted passages from the writings of Moses and all the prophets, explaining what all the Scriptures said about himself.

[28]By this time they were nearing Emmaus and the end of their journey. Jesus would have gone on, [29]but they begged him to stay the night with them, since it was getting late. So he went home with them. [30]As they sat down to eat, he took a small loaf of bread, asked God's blessing on it, broke it, then gave it to them. [31]Suddenly, their eyes were opened, and they recognized him. And at that moment he disappeared!

³² They said to each other, "Didn't our hearts feel strangely warm as he talked with us on the road and explained the Scriptures to us?" ³³ And within the hour they were on their way back to Jerusalem, where the eleven disciples and the other followers of Jesus were gathered. When they arrived, they were greeted with the report, ³⁴ "The Lord has really risen! He appeared to Peter*!"

Jesus Appears to the Disciples

³⁵ Then the two from Emmaus told their story of how Jesus had appeared to them as they were walking along the road and how they had recognized him as he was breaking the bread. ³⁶ And just as they were telling about it, Jesus himself was suddenly standing there among them. He said, "Peace be with you."* ³⁷ But the whole group was terribly frightened, thinking they were seeing a ghost! ³⁸ "Why are you frightened?" he asked. "Why do you doubt who I am? ³⁹ Look at my hands. Look at my feet. You can see that it's really me. Touch me and make sure that I am not a ghost, because ghosts don't have bodies, as you see that I do!" ⁴⁰ As he spoke, he held out his hands for them to see, and he showed them his feet.*

⁴¹ Still they stood there doubting, filled with joy and wonder. Then he asked them, "Do you have anything here to eat?" ⁴² They gave him a piece of broiled fish, ⁴³ and he ate it as they watched.

⁴⁴ Then he said, "When I was with you before, I told you that everything written about me by Moses and the prophets and in the Psalms must all come true." ⁴⁵ Then he opened their minds to understand these many Scriptures. ⁴⁶ And he said, "Yes, it was written long ago

that the Messiah must suffer and die and rise again from the dead on the third day. [47] With my authority, take this message of repentance to all the nations, beginning in Jerusalem: 'There is forgiveness of sins for all who turn to me.' [48] You are witnesses of all these things.

[49] "And now I will send the Holy Spirit, just as my Father promised. But stay here in the city until the Holy Spirit comes and fills you with power from heaven."

The Ascension

[50] Then Jesus led them to Bethany, and lifting his hands to heaven, he blessed them. [51] While he was blessing them, he left them and was taken up to heaven.* [52] They worshipped him and* then returned to Jerusalem filled with great joy. [53] And they spent all of their time in the Temple, praising God.

Footnotes

Chapter 1

1:1 Or *have been fulfilled.*
1:15 Or *even from birth.*
1:17 See Mal 4:5–6.
1:28 Some manuscripts add *Blessed are you among women.*
1:33 Greek *over the house of Jacob.*

Chapter 2

2:14 Or *and peace on earth for all those pleasing God;* some manuscripts read *and peace on earth, goodwill among people.*
2:23 Exod 13:2
2:24 Lev 12:8
2:49 Or *"Didn't you realize that I should be involved with my Father's affairs?"*

Chapter 3

3:1a Greek *Herod was tetrarch.* Herod Antipas was a son of King Herod.
3:1b Greek *tetrarch;* also in 3:1c, 19.
3:3 Greek *preaching a baptism of repentance for the forgiveness of sins.*
3:4–6 Isa 40:3–5
3:16a Or *in.*
3:16b Greek *to untie his sandals.*
3:16c Or *in the Holy Spirit and in fire.*
3:22 Some manuscripts read *and today I have become your Father.*
3:32 Greek *Sala;* see Ruth 4:22.
3:33 *Arni* is the same person as Ram; see 1 Chr 2:9–10.
3:38 Greek *Enos;* see Gen 5:6.

Chapter 4

4:4 Deut 8:3
4:8 Deut 6:13
4:10–11 Ps 91:11–12
4:12 Deut 6:16
4:18–19 Or *and to proclaim the acceptable year of the Lord.* Isa 61:1–2.
4:44 Some manuscripts read *Galilee.*

Chapter 5

5:1 Greek *Lake Gennesaret,* another name for the Sea of Galilee.
5:3 *Simon* is called *Peter* in 6:14 and thereafter.
5:30 Greek *with tax collectors and sinners.*

Chapter 6

6:41 Greek *your brother's eye;* also in 6:42.
6:42 Greek *Brother.*

Chapter 7

7:23 Or *who don't fall away because of me.*
7:27 Mal 3:1
7:29 Or *praised God.*
7:35 Or *But wisdom is justified by all her children.*
7:37 Greek *an alabaster jar.*
7:41 Greek *500 denarii.* A denarius was the equivalent of a full day's wage.

Chapter 8

8:10 Isa 6:9
8:26 Some manuscripts read *Gadarenes;* other manuscripts read *Gergesenes.* See Matt 8:28; Mark 5:1.
8:43 Some manuscripts omit *She had spent everything she had on doctors.*

Chapter 9

9:7 Greek *Herod the tetrarch.* He was a son of King Herod and was ruler over one of the four districts in Palestine.
9:33 Or *shelters;* Greek reads *tabernacles.*
9:35 Some manuscripts read *This is my beloved Son.*
9:54 Some manuscripts add *as Elijah did.*
9:55 Some manuscripts add *And he said, "You don't realize what your hearts are like. 56For the Son of Man has not come to destroy men's lives, but to save them."*
9:60 Greek *Let the dead bury their own dead.*

Chapter 10

10:1 Some manuscripts read *70*; also in 10:17.
10:15 Greek *to Hades.*
10:27 Deut 6:5; Lev 19:18.
10:32 Greek *A Levite.*
10:35 Greek *2 denarii.* A denarius was the equivalent of a full day's wage.

Chapter 11

11:2–4 Some manuscripts add additional portions of the Lord's Prayer as it reads in Matt 6:9–13.
11:8 Greek *in order to avoid shame,* or *because of [your] persistence.*
11:11 Some manuscripts add *for bread, do you give them a stone? Or if they ask.*
11:15 Greek *Beelzeboul.*
11:18 Greek *by Beelzeboul;* also in 11:19.
11:21 Greek *the strong one.*
11:31 Greek *the queen of the south.*
11:42 Greek *to tithe the mint and the rue and every herb.*
11:49 Greek *Therefore, the wisdom of God said.*

Chapter 12

12:38 Greek *in the second or third watch.*

Chapter 13

13:16 Greek *this woman, a daughter of Abraham.*
13:21 Greek *3 measures.*
13:30 Greek *Some are last who will be first, and some are first who will be last.*
13:35 Ps 118:26

Chapter 14

14:2 Traditionally translated *who had dropsy.*
14:5 Some manuscripts read *donkey.*
14:26 Greek *you must hate.*

Chapter 15

15:8 Greek *10 drachmas.* A drachma was the equivalent of a full day's wage.
15:21 Some manuscripts add *Please take me on as a hired man.*

Chapter 16

16:6 Greek *100 baths . . . 50 [baths]*.
16:7 Greek *100 korous . . . 80 [korous]*.
16:9 Or *Then when you run out at the end of this life, your friends will welcome you into eternal homes*.
16:22 Greek *into Abraham's bosom*.
16:23 Greek *to Hades*.

Chapter 17

17:3 Greek *your brother*.
17:20 Or *by your speculations*.
17:21 Or *within you*.
17:25 Or *suffer many things*.
17:30 Or *on the day the Son of Man is revealed*.
17:31 Greek *on the roof*.
17:35 Some manuscripts add verse 36, *Two men will be working in the field; one will be taken, the other left*.
17:37 Greek *Wherever the carcass is, the vultures gather*.

Chapter 18

18:20 Exod 20:12–16; Deut 5:16–20.

Chapter 19

19:13 Greek *10 minas*, about 6 kilograms or 12.5 pounds in weight. 1 mina was worth about 3 months' wages.
19:26 Or *who have nothing*.
19:38 Pss 118:26; 148:1.
19:46 Isa 56:7; Jer 7:11.

Chapter 20

20:2 Or *By whose authority do you do these things?*
20:17 Ps 118:22
20:24 Greek *a denarius*.
20:28 Deut 25:5–6
20:37a Greek *when he wrote about the bush. He referred to the Lord*.
20:37b Exod 3:6
20:42–43 Ps 110:1

Chapter 21

21:2 Greek *2 lepta.*
21:8 Greek *name, saying, 'I am.'*
21:27 See Dan 7:13.
21:32 Or *this age,* or *this nation.*

Chapter 22

22:19-20 Some manuscripts omit 22:19b-20, *given for you . . . I will pour out for you.*
22:37 Isa 53:12
22:43-44 These verses are not included in many ancient manuscripts.
22:66 Greek *before their Sanhedrin.*
22:69 See Ps 110:1.

Chapter 23

23:16 Some manuscripts add verse 17, *For it was necessary for him to release one [prisoner] for them during the feast.*
23:26 *Cyrene* was a city in northern Africa.
23:31 Or *If these things are done to me, the living tree, what will happen to you, the dry tree?*
23:33 Sometimes rendered *Calvary,* which comes from the Latin word for "skull."
23:34a This sentence is not included in many ancient manuscripts.
23:34b Greek *by casting lots.* See Ps 22:18.
23:46 Ps 31:5
23:47 Or *righteous.*
23:48 Greek *beating their breasts.*
23:54 Greek *on the day of preparation.*

Chapter 24

24:1 Greek *But on the first day of the week, very early in the morning.*
24:12 Some manuscripts do not include this verse.
24:13 Greek *60 stadia [7 miles].*
24:34 Greek *Simon.*
24:36 Some manuscripts do not include *He said, "Peace be with you."*
24:40 Some manuscripts do not include this verse.
24:51 Some manuscripts do not include *and was taken up to heaven.*
24:52 Some manuscripts do not include *worshipped him and.*

Notes:

Notes:

Notes:

Notes:

Notes:

Notes: